ST NEOTS
PAST

St Neots High Street in about 1900.

ST NEOTS PAST

Rosa Young

Phillimore

1996

Published by
PHILLIMORE & CO. LTD.,
Shopwyke Manor Barn, Chichester, West Sussex

ISBN 1 86077 025 8

Printed and bound in Great Britain by
BIDDLES LTD.
Guildford, Surrey

Contents

List of Illustrations

Frontispiece: High Street, *c*.1900

Acknowledgements

The author wishes to thank the following for permission to reproduce illustrations.

Mr. D. Bushby, 32; Cambridge Antiquarian Society, 8, 9, 10, 15, 17; Cambridge University Committee for Aerial Photography, 7; County Record Office, Huntingdon, 28, 36, 37, 38, 67, 77, 86, 87, 88, 90, 94, 124, 131, 142, 143; Mr. L. Forscutt, frontispiece, 31, 42, 51, 66, 79, 83-5, 104, 109, 112, 115, 120, 126-28, 134-37, 139; Longsands Museum, St Neots, 4-6, 27, 48, 96, 103; Norris Museum and Library, St Ives, 70, 81, 82, 92, 108; Mrs. L. Reed, 21, 34, 41, 46, 47, 61, 62, 89, 100, 113, 117, 149; Mr. M. Richardson, 101; St Neots Local History Society, 2, 3, 19, 20, 22, 24-6, 55, 64, 65, 75, 76, 78, 93, 106, 122, 133, 141, 144, 145; St Neots Museum Trust, 1, 13, 14, 40, 43, 44, 49, 50, 56, 58, 63, 68, 69, 71, 74, 80, 91, 95, 98, 107, 110, 111, 114, 121, 132, 138, 140, 147, 148; Phillimore and Co. Ltd., 97.

Thanks also to staff at St Neots Branch Library, County Record Offices at Huntingdon and Bedford, and members of St Neots Local History Society for assistance with research.

Introduction

St Neots is a town on the River Ouse, roughly equidistant from Huntingdon to the north-east and Bedford to the south-west. It derives its name from a Saxon saint whose bones once rested in its priory.

As now constituted, the town consists of four elements. The medieval market town of St Neots was joined by the adjacent village of Eynesbury in 1876 and the villages of Eaton Socon and Eaton Ford were absorbed in 1965. This amalgamation, together with an increase in population resulting from a London Overspill Agreement in the 1960s and county boundary changes in 1974, means that St Neots grew from a modest market town in Huntingdonshire to become the third largest conurbation in Cambridgeshire, surpassed only by Cambridge and Peterborough.

In spite of all the changes which have occurred, each of the constituent parts of St Neots retains its own character and has its own distinctive history, a summary of which is told in the chapters which follow.

Chapter 1

The Early History

It is difficult to imagine what the St Neots area must have looked like about five thousand years ago. The river was there, of course, and the tributaries leading to it, but the river was wider and shallower than it is now, with marshy edges full of rushes and reeds. Beyond that on either side was probably grassland with, further back, the grass punctuated by bushes and trees. On high ground even further back the trees would have been more numerous, developing into dense woodland, thick with undergrowth and full of wild animals.

Into this wilderness came the Hunter-Gatherers, so called because they hunted animals and gathered wild fruits and berries. They are believed to have been nomadic people, never staying very long in any one place and erecting only temporary shelters in which to sleep for one or two nights.

Needless to say no trace of these shelters remains, but what the Hunter-Gatherers may have left behind is the pattern of roads and paths that we use now. Hunters would probably have made their way through the tall grass near the river,

1   The River Ouse, an essential element in the history of St Neots.

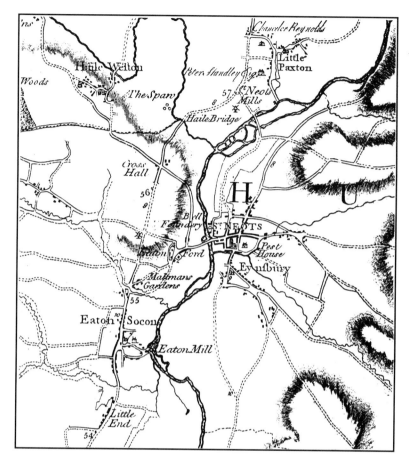

2 Part of Jeffreys' map of Huntingdonshire, 1768, showing the pattern of roads in the St Neots area.

lurking there to catch their quarry as the animals came down to drink. In this way tracks parallel to the river would form, at least in the summer months. In winter the river would have flooded— as it still does—and the grassland tracks would have been unusable, so a second route would have been needed. This was probably on higher ground, perhaps just within the edges of the woodland. Sometimes travellers would have needed to cross the river, perhaps walking along the tributary valleys and heading for places where it was easy to wade across the water.

Once tracks were established in this way they may have continued in use over many centuries, becoming accepted as traditional routes. A glance at the pattern of principal roads in the region of St Neots appears to support this theory. Winter tracks could have resulted in the routes taken by the Great North Road west of the river and Huntingdon Street—Church Street—Barford Road to the east. One summer route may have been roughly on the line of the road across St Neots Common, another could have been the basis for the lower end of Crosshall Road. Cross tracks leading to the river may survive as parts of Cambridge Street, which runs alongside Fox Brook, and Howitts Lane beside Henbrook. On an 18th-century map a road by Duloe Brook at Eaton Socon is marked and other cross tracks may once have led to river-crossings at Eaton Socon Mill and Little Paxton.

By about 3000 B.C., when the Stone Age began, there was probably a well-used network of double trackways running parallel to the river on both sides, crossed by other tracks which converged on suitable river-crossing points. It is believed to have been during the Neolithic period, or New Stone Age, that the first small settlements were established. The most important factor in selecting a suitable site was the proximity of a good water supply so the river and its tributaries would have attracted early settlers. It is also likely that they would have chosen a place close to a trackway, perhaps at a point where two tracks crossed, and probably on a winter rather than a summer route. The likely sites at St Neots would be somewhere near The Cross at the eastern end of High Street, and at the northern end of Huntingdon Street where it meets Mill Lane and Priory Hill. At Eynesbury the settlement could have been near the junction of Howitts Lane with Berkley Street, or perhaps further south. At Eaton Socon there are several possible sites along the Great North Road—at Bushmead Road corner, at the School Lane corner and further south in the region of Little End. Eaton Ford has crossroads at Mill Hill and Crosshall, both possible sites for settlement.

Evidence of Neolithic occupation is very scarce locally. Traces of a Neolithic hearth were found at Little End, Eaton Socon in 1948 but apart from that the only finds so far have been a few flint tools and weapons, mostly hand axes, in isolated locations.

There is ample evidence of occupation of these sites during the Bronze Age from 2000 B.C. to 500 B.C. and during the Iron Age which followed. At Eaton Ford, near the Crosshall crossroads, a Bronze-Age site yielded a socketed axe and two spiral finger rings and an Iron-Age site in the same area, excavated by G.T. Rudd in the early 1970s, revealed an unusual pentagonal structure. The evidence suggested that it had been timber-framed and very large and in his report Mr. Rudd referred to the fact that polygonal temples had been found on similar sites elsewhere, which may explain its purpose. Iron-Age sites have also been discovered near Bushmead Road in Eaton Socon and in the Wyboston Lakes area further south.

In 1889 Mr. Harvey of Eynesbury unearthed several fragments of Bronze-Age pottery and two polished stone axes from a gravel pit behind the Red House in Montagu Square, and in more recent times C.F. Tebbutt found

sherds of pottery of Iron-Age date in the area between Eynesbury Rectory and the river. A late Iron-Age settlement also existed near Howitts Lane, traces of which were discovered in 1966 by G.T. Rudd and C. Daines.

A dig conducted by C.F. Tebbutt in the grounds of Old Hall Place off Church Street, St Neots in 1929 revealed deposits which included bronze and iron objects underlying later levels, suggesting that there was a community living near The Cross in the Bronze and Iron Ages, and there was almost certainly a Bronze-Age settlement close to the crossroads at the northern end of Huntingdon Street. Aerial photographs show the cropmarks of circular ditches in two fields which are probably the shadows of Bronze-Age round burial mounds, known as barrows, indicating a settlement

3 Fragments of Bronze-Age pottery found in 1889 at The Coneygeare, Eynesbury.

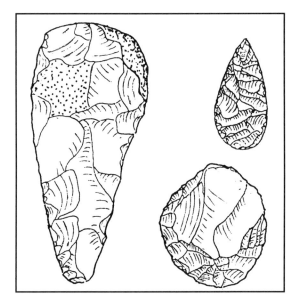

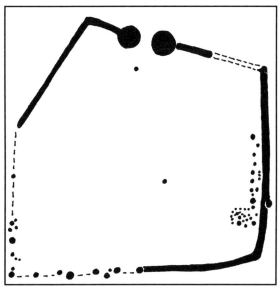

4 Above left. *Stone-Age implements found at St Neots. Left: Palaeolithic hand axe. Top right: Neolithic arrowhead. Bottom right: Neolithic scraper. (From a drawing by G.T. Rudd.)*

5 Above right. *Plan of pentagonal Iron-Age building, Crosshall, Eaton Ford. (From a drawing by G.T. Rudd.)*

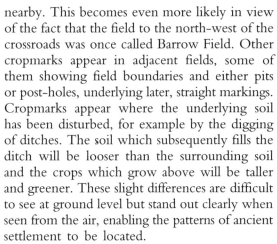

6 Left. *Spiral bronze finger ring from a site at Crosshall, Eaton Ford. (From a drawing by G.T. Rudd.)*

nearby. This becomes even more likely in view of the fact that the field to the north-west of the crossroads was once called Barrow Field. Other cropmarks appear in adjacent fields, some of them showing field boundaries and either pits or post-holes, underlying later, straight markings. Cropmarks appear where the underlying soil has been disturbed, for example by the digging of ditches. The soil which subsequently fills the ditch will be looser than the surrounding soil and the crops which grow above will be taller and greener. These slight differences are difficult to see at ground level but stand out clearly when seen from the air, enabling the patterns of ancient settlement to be located.

By the time the Romans made their first tentative invasion of Britain in 55 B.C. the St Neots area was thinly populated with several small villages and hamlets. The people would have been living in simple circular huts with mud walls and thatched or turf roofs. Little is known about their social organisation but it is likely that there were local chiefs to make the rules and religious leaders to regulate the ceremonies by which they honoured the pagan gods which they worshipped. By the end of the first century B.C. the local landscape would have altered considerably because woodland had been felled and scrub cleared to create space for farms and villages.

The Romans arrived in earnest in A.D. 43. Their well-trained and organised soldiers had little trouble overcoming the Iron-Age warriors of Britain and they succeeded in becoming the ruling class, either by conquest or by negotiation. As the Romans were predominantly town-dwellers, they set about building towns and good roads to link them. Two towns were established at Godmanchester in Huntingdonshire and at Sandy in Bedfordshire and the road which linked them is marked on Ordnance Survey maps, running in a north-south direction to the east of the railway line at St Neots. Only short stretches of it remain incorporated into the present road system but it survives here and there as a footpath or farm road. G.C. Gorham in his history of St Neots published in 1824, claimed that another Roman road parallel to this ran along the eastern parish boundary of St Neots, passing through Weald and not far from Monks Hardwick Farm. He referred to observations by Rev. B. Hutchinson in 1796 concerning ditches and 'five or six tumuli' to the west of the road, near the farm.

7   *Aerial photograph of Barrow Field area, St Neots, showing cropmarks, looking south with Priory Park upper left. Reproduced by permission of Cambridge University Committee for Aerial Photography.*

Several years ago a group of researchers calling themselves The Viatores claimed to have traced several other Roman roads in the area, one of which was on the line of the main road from Cambridge to St Neots. It was shown on a conjectural map as veering off beyond Eltisley to pass through St Neots to the north of the present High Street, although the course indicated was rather vague. One 18th-century map of the county and two 19th-century maps, the latter perhaps based on earlier sources, showed a road which once existed as a continuation north-westwards of Kings Lane. A river crossing lining up with its projected route would also line up with the upper end of Crosshall Road and the road to Hail Weston. This may have been the true route of the road partially traced by The Viatores, as the stretch west of Crosshall was called 'Stanestrete' in the Middle Ages, a name associated with Roman roads.

The Viatores also found traces of a Roman road passing through Bushmead and Basmead in the parish of Eaton Socon. At Bushmead Priory it appeared to cross another road coming from the south-west and heading towards Godmanchester. C.F. Tebbutt found evidence of a Roman road in the vicinity of Howitts Lane, Eynesbury, and there are doubtless more roads in the region which await discovery.

Most of the signs of Roman occupation in the St Neots area come from Eynesbury. In 1933 C.F. Tebbutt found the earthworks of a Roman encampment near the river, south of The Coneygeare, where it may have been set up to guard a river-crossing. More recently G.T. Rudd discovered traces of a small Roman villa with hypocaust heating close by, perhaps the home of the camp commander. G.C. Gorham's book mentions 'lines of entrenchment' being visible on the camp site during the 19th century and adds that within them there was 'an artificial mound' at that time. Numerous Roman coins have been found on or near this site over several centuries, including those of Domitian, Hadrian and Constantinius, covering a period from the first to the fourth centuries A.D.

Also at Eynesbury, in the late Iron-Age settlement already mentioned, G.T. Rudd and C. Daines found a Roman cremation burial. It

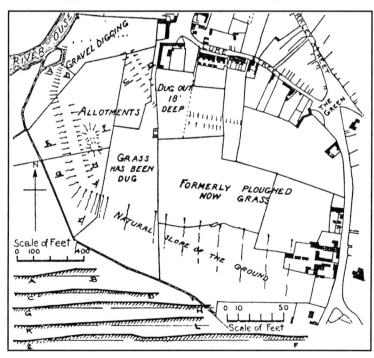

8 Plan of earthworks of Roman encampment to the south of The Coneygeare, Eynesbury. (From V.C.H. Hunts., 1932)

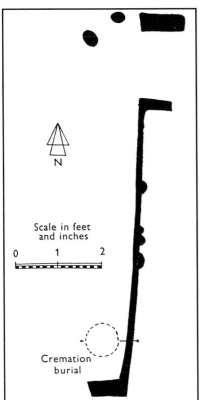

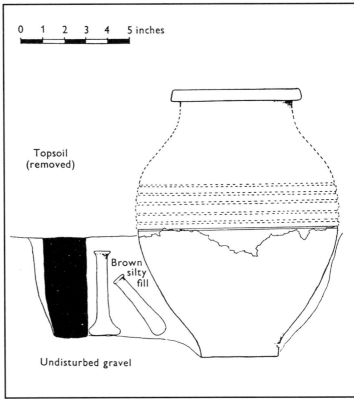

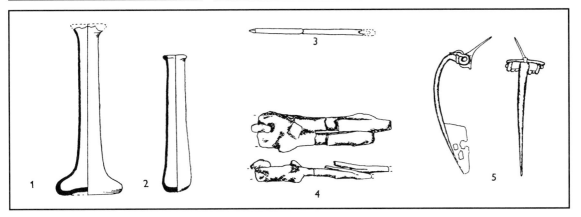

9   *Diagram of Roman cremation burial and artifacts, Brickhills Estate, Eynesbury.*

consisted of a whiteware pot containing human bones, together with two small glass bottles, one of which contained powder and a bone needle. The burial had been partly enclosed by a timber structure painted orange and also on the site were scraps of pottery dating from about 50 B.C. to the second century A.D.

Some evidence of Roman presence in St Neots was discovered in the course of excavations to the south-east of The Cross, in the form of pieces of pottery of the third and fourth centuries A.D., scattered over a wide area, but so far no major discoveries have been made within the town.

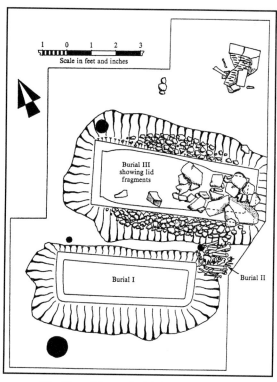

1 0 1 2 3
Scale in feet and inches

Burial III
showing lid
fragments

Burial I

Burial II

10 *Plan of Roman burial site at Eaton Ford.*

At Eaton Socon aerial photographs revealed the cropmarks of a Roman villa to the north of the parish church and east of the Great North Road, perhaps connected with a river-crossing nearby, but there is no record of any Roman finds from this site. At Eaton Ford two Roman stone coffins were excavated by Rudd and Daines in Windmill Field, west of the main road. Pottery from the third and fourth centuries was found on the site, together with scraps of hypocaust tile and fragments of the tesserae used for making mosaics. These were spread over a wide area, suggesting the former presence of either one large building or several smaller ones. The coffins had been desecrated during a later Roman period, perhaps by robbers suspecting the inclusion of valuable grave goods. In view of the stone coffins and the mosaics, the deceased persons were probably wealthy, so they may

have been right. The Roman burials had themselves disturbed burials from an earlier period, so the site may have been occupied continuously at least from the Bronze Age.

The native inhabitants of the St Neots area were probably engaged in growing crops to feed their Roman overlords and may have produced sufficient quantity to supply nearby towns as well. Some years ago dredging operations in the river near the bridge at Little Paxton fished up a number of timbers dating from the Roman period. They could once have been part of a landing stage or jetty where local produce was loaded onto boats for transport by water to Godmanchester and other Roman towns.

The early history of St Neots is therefore probably one of gradual development over a very long period of time, with small groups clearing more and more woodland and scrub to create farms and village sites as communities expanded. Routes through the region became established, some of them linking with neighbouring settlements being established at Huntingdon and Cambridge. There are no major earthworks in the vicinity of St Neots, which suggests that the inhabitants did not fear attack from other tribes or communities, and the Roman invaders were probably accepted into the community with resignation rather than resistance. The Romans improved the road system and brought a more efficient form of administration but the urbanisation which affected some other parts of the county does not seem to have happened at St Neots and it remained a rural community.

It should be emphasised, however, that much of this chapter is conjectural and the limited evidence for early historical periods is capable of being interpreted in many ways. Each new archaeological find adds something new to our knowledge but a clearer picture is impossible without demolishing all the buildings in St Neots, Eynesbury and the Eatons to see what lies beneath.

Chapter 2

Anglo-Saxon Eynesbury and Eaton

The Romans, having spread themselves too widely and too thinly, found themselves in trouble and began withdrawing from the outskirts of their empire. They abandoned Britain between A.D. 446 and A.D. 454, leaving the field open for other invaders who had been infiltrating the country even before the Romans left.

These newcomers were the Angles, Saxons and Jutes from across the Channel. The Jutes, who settled mainly in Kent, were evidently in the minority because the period which followed is referred to as the Anglo-Saxon period. Judging by its name, East Anglia was principally settled by the Angles, but as St Neots is on the western borders of that region it was probably occupied by a mixture of Angles and Saxons.

It was once popularly supposed that the Anglo-Saxons drove all the resident Britons, also known as Celts, westwards into Wales, Ireland and Cornwall but that is now thought to be an over-simplification of events. There may have been some migration but the likely facts are that Saxon influence was slower to spread to the western extremities of the British Isles, enabling the native Celts there to retain much of their own culture. Other British Celts probably stayed put, living alongside the newcomers and eventually being absorbed into their way of life. That this may have happened locally is suggested by the place-name evidence.

We do not know what the Celts called the places where they lived because in most cases we only know towns and villages by the names that were given to them by the Anglo-Saxons. The only Celtic names which have survived are river names. The River Ouse, for example, derives its name from a Celtic word meaning 'water'. Our other local names are all Anglo-Saxon in origin.

On the eastern side of the river a Saxon called Ernulf, Eynulf or Ainulf evidently took over the abandoned Roman camp near the river-crossing. The Anglo-Saxon word for a fortified place was *burgh* or *byrig* and the new community which became established there was called Eanulfesbyrig, then Einulvesberie and eventually Eynesbury. On the other hand the settlement further north, by the crossroads that would become The Cross in St Neots, was not given an Anglo-Saxon name, which could mean that it remained a British Celtic village for a time. The only traces of early Anglo-Saxon settlement so far discovered in the St Neots town area were in Avenue Road, further north, where

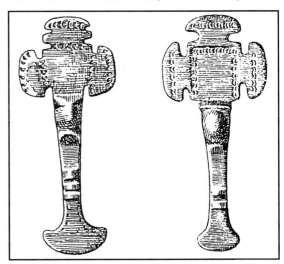

11 Two pre-Christian Anglo-Saxon brooches found in Avenue Road, St Neots in 1886, in association with burials. (From V.C.H. Hunts., 1932)

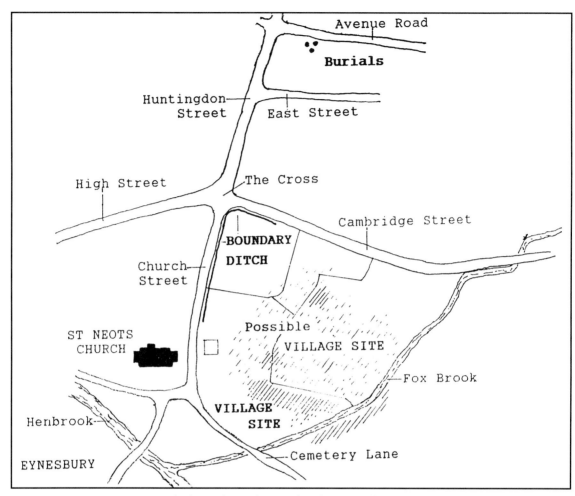

12 *Sketch map showing location of Anglo-Saxon village, St Neots.*

several burials were unearthed in 1886. Two of the skeletons which were found had spears buried with them, and a number of other artifacts including brooches, a knife and harness fittings were also found. The brooches are on display in the Norris Museum at St Ives but all the other items were dispersed and lost. It may be that the earliest Anglo-Saxons to come to the area settled in the region of Avenue Road at first because the prime site at the crossroads was already occupied.

On the west bank of the river a Saxon, or a group of Saxons, established or took over a farm or village near the water's edge. The Anglo-Saxon word for water was *ea* and the word *tun*

was used indiscriminately for farm, homestead or village, hence *Ea-tun* and then Eaton. To the north of this settlement the river crossing area became *forda* then Ford and it retained that simple name for many centuries, the prefix Eaton only being added much later. On the hilltop above Ford, at the crossroads, the settlement was evidently also fortified as its name, Sudbury, means the south fortified place.

Information about the early Anglo-Saxon period is scanty, and most of it is conjectural, based on archaeological evidence. The general history of the time, The Anglo-Saxon Chronicle, is a fascinating but frustrating mixture of fact and fantasy that cannot always be relied on, and few other documentary sources have survived. Presumably the newcomers were able to dominate the scene fairly rapidly and comprehensively since it is to the Anglo-Saxons that we owe our language, our administrative structure, our class system and our laws. It was the Anglo-Saxons who also defined the counties and their sub-divisions, and the boundaries of individual estates or manors. They established parish boundaries too, when they had embraced Christianity.

The sub-divisions of counties in this part of England are known as Hundreds. At one time they were important units of local administration but nowadays they are only used as convenient groupings for electoral purposes. The word 'Hundred' may have arisen because each area consisted of a hundred hides, a hide being a rather nebulous acreage of land which could be ploughed in one day by a team of oxen. It could also have meant the amount of land occupied by a hundred families or farms and opinion is divided. St Neots and Eynesbury are in the Hundred of Toseland and Eaton, having been part of Bedfordshire, is in Barford Hundred.

Because Toseland village bears the name of the Hundred, it is sometimes suspected that it must once have been a much larger village, but that is not the case. Meetings of the Hundred, called 'moots', were held regularly and were attended by representatives from all its constituent villages and hamlets. As this involved a large number of people the moots were held in the open air, at a traditional meeting place, often marked by a large stone or some prominent natural feature. The other Huntingdonshire Hundreds are Hursting*stone*, Leighton*stone* and Norman *Cross*. In the case of Toseland the moots were held near the sacred grove or *lundr* belonging to a man called Toli and the name of the meeting place was Toli's lundr, and eventually Toseland.

The Anglo-Saxons worshipped pagan gods when they first came to this country, which may partially explain the relatively tolerant acceptance of these newcomers by the British Celts, as they too were pagans. There were,

nevertheless, pockets of Christianity surviving in some parts of the country, left over from the Roman occupation as the Romans had been converted to Christianity before they left Britain. The Pope in Rome, dismayed at the return to paganism following the Roman withdrawal, sent Augustine and several other missionaries to Britain in A.D. 597 with orders to re-convert the English. This mission was successful and by the end of the seventh century East Anglia and much of the rest of the country was nominally Christian.

From then onwards churches were built, priests ordained and parishes defined. At first only a few churches were built, serving very large parishes, and these were known as minsters or mother churches. They housed several priests who went out to outlying communities within the parish to preach at open air services. Eaton probably had a mother church because its parish has always been extensive, the largest in acreage of all the parishes in Bedfordshire. It encompassed Bushmead, Staploe, Duloe, Honeydon, Begwary, Colesden, Chawston and Wyboston. It is not known whether the first church at Eaton was a timber one or was stone-built, or whether it was sited on the same spot as the present one or was built nearer the river.

On the other side of the Ouse the early church was at Great Paxton. Although considerably altered in later centuries the church there still has its Anglo-Saxon columns on both sides of the nave and forming its crossing arches. It is known to have been a mother church with several priests who travelled to Little Paxton, Toseland and probably Abbotsley. The Abbotsley connection appears to be confirmed by the fact that an old route between the villages was known until the 17th century as Abbotsley Way, and at Great Paxton church one of the doorways was known as the Abbotsley door.

It is likely that Eynesbury was originally part of Great Paxton parish too, since it lies between there and Abbotsley, but if so it evidently broke away at quite an early stage, since there is no tradition of any connection, and there was a church at Eynesbury by the late Anglo-Saxon

Great Paxton Church, St. Neots.

13   Great Paxton church, originally an Anglo-Saxon minster.

period. As time progressed many outlying villages in these large parishes built their own churches, acquired a resident priest and became separate parishes. In some cases they still operated under the control of the mother church, having to attend some services there and pay fees to it. They were usually allowed to perform baptisms but not marriages or burial services. The churches at Toseland and Little Paxton maintained their dependence on the mother church at Great Paxton until comparatively recent years, and are still closely linked, but Abbotsley and Eynesbury achieved total independence.

The parish of Eynesbury included what is now St Neots, together with several small hamlets such as Hardwick and 'Cotes', which was probably Caldecote, to the south and Weald and Wintringham to the east. The church at Eynesbury was probably on the same site as the present one, with the houses of the villagers clustered round it. The parish was mainly divided into two large manors, each owned by a different Saxon earl. The manor to the south, corresponding with what is still Eynesbury, had the parish church in it and it may have been that fact which prompted the lord of the manor to the north, that which we now call St Neots, into his decision to found a monastery and go one better than his neighbour! Depending on which document you favour, this ambitious earl was either called Alric with a wife called Ethelfleda, or he was Leofric and his wife Leofleda. To simplify matters he will be referred to as Leofric.

Leofric applied to the abbey which was then at Ely for permission to establish a religious house on his manor, to be under the authority of Ely Abbey. Consent was given and some monks were sent from Ely to give Leofric a start and in that way the first priory was founded and was dedicated in A.D. 974. So far there is no definite evidence to show where Leofric built his priory. One theory is that it was situated on the same riverside site as the later Norman priory, but others have held the opinion that it was built further east, near The Cross, perhaps even at the place where the parish church now stands. One contemporary document described the priory as having been built next to the earl's manor house, and that may have been within the triangle formed by Cambridge Street, Church Street and Fox Brook, near The Cross.

In 1961 P.V. Addyman conducted an archaeological dig in the southern part of this area and found evidence of a number of Anglo-Saxon buildings. One of them was described as measuring 25 ft. by 40 ft. and probably having cills and joists to support a wooden floor. This suggests a building of some status as most houses of the period had earth floors and it could be that it was Leofric's manor house. It was a one-roomed hall, boat shaped with walls curving in slightly so that it was narrower at both ends than in the middle. Mr. Addyman, referring to the lack of Anglo-Saxon material on the riverside priory site, was one of those in favour of this Church Street area being the probable location of the first priory.

14 *Gated entrance to Old Hall Place, Church Street, photographed in about 1895. The Anglo-Saxon village was discovered in the area beyond.*

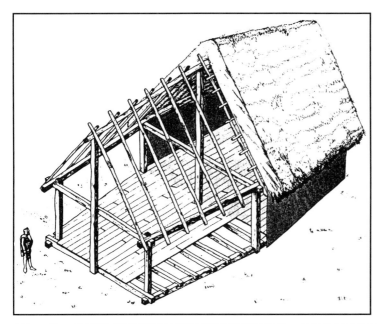

15 Left. Sketch showing possible construction of Anglo-Saxon building, foundations of which were found on Church Street site in 1961.

16 Below left. Anglo-Saxon pottery from Church Street site, found 1930s. (Based on a photograph in V.C.H. Hunts., 1932.)

17 Below right. Objects found on Church Street site, 1930s. 1. Axe. 2. Bone handle. 3. Part of grip of shield boss. 4. Fragment of comb. 5. Iron knife.

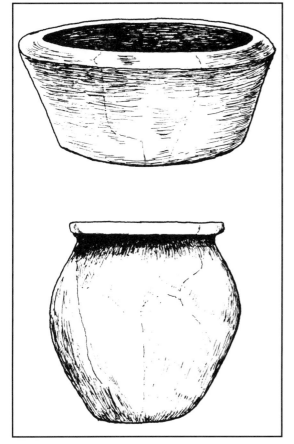

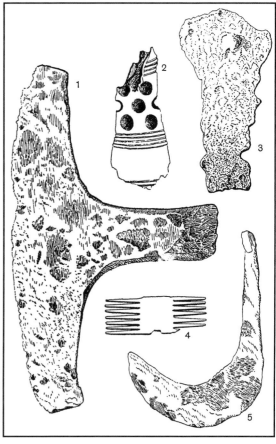

A few years later, in 1964, C.F. Tebbutt traced a ditch of Anglo-Saxon date running along the south side of Cambridge Street and the east side of Church Street which partially enclosed the settlement found by Mr. Addyman. This ditch could have been the re-digging of defences which originally surrounded the British Celtic settlement there. Perhaps when the newcomers took it over they strengthened the ditches as a precaution against reprisals!

Other evidence from further north on the same site was found by Mr. Tebbutt in 1929. Several pits and a number of artifacts were suggestive of workshops and sunken huts. Two of the pits, one of them seven feet in length, had fireholes and remains of metal slag within them. Also among the finds were part of a stone quern for grinding grain, a simple plough-share and the clay rings which served as loom-weights when weaving. Pieces of the wattle and daub used in building houses, and pieces of pottery were scattered all over the site. Another investigation in 1932 revealed more pits and an iron axe dated between A.D. 650 and A.D. 850.

It seems likely therefore that Leofric's village, manor house and priory were situated on the east side of Church Street, near the junction where the road from Cambridge crosses the road from Huntingdon, a logical place for a Saxon earl to establish his residence. There is no evidence so far to indicate that there were buildings any further west than this.

Once Leofric had built his priory he wanted a relic to put in it. Many religious houses boasted some item that had reputedly been associated with a saint or one of the Holy Family, such as a piece of clothing or a bone or something else with religious significance. What Leofric coveted was the entire body of Saint Neot, a much revered Saxon monk who had spent much of his life in Cornwall and who had died and been buried there in about A.D. 875.

Neot is thought by some historians to have been related to King Alfred the Great, and he was certainly a favourite of the king. Alfred is reported as carrying into battle with him a banner bearing a likeness of St Neot and there is a legend which tells how Neot appeared to the king in a dream during the night before one important battle, assuring him of his support and promising victory. The famous Alfred Jewel, found in 1693, is thought to depict St Neot. It is made of gold, enamel and crystal and shows the upper part of a figure holding two staffs

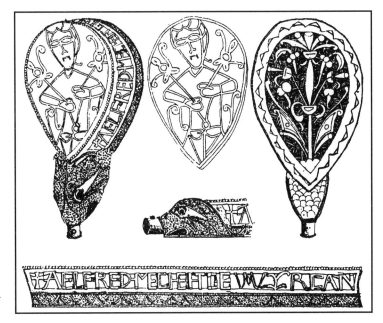

18   *The Alfred Jewel. (From G.C. Gorham's* History of St Neots, *1824.)*

19 The village of St Neot in Cornwall.

with foliate ends. Round its edges are the words 'AELFRED MEC HEHT GEWYRCAN' which means 'Alfred had me made'.

According to one of his biographers Neot had been a soldier who renounced a life of violence in favour of one of contemplation and worship. He became a monk at Glastonbury Abbey where he rose to be Sacristan, but he later sought a solitary life, becoming a hermit in Cornwall. Other monks joined him after a time and Neot presided over a small religious house near the village which was then called Hamstoke or Guerrirs-stoke, on the edge of Bodmin Moor. After he died his body was preserved in a shrine there and the village was named Neot-stoke, and later St Neot, in his memory.

Many stories were written about the saint, most of them considerably fictionalised to make the events appear to have been miracles. St Neot was apparently a very short man—less than three feet tall according to one writer— and he had difficulty in reaching the latch of the door at Glastonbury Abbey. During his time as Sacristan there he was roused late one night to admit a visitor when no helpers were about to open up for him, whereupon the latch slid miraculously down the door until it was within his reach! The tale is also told of a miraculous fish pond in Cornwall that was given to him and which always contained two fishes as long as only one was removed at any one time. However, on one occasion when

St Neot was ill in bed his servant took out both fishes and cooked them for the saint's meal. Neot was highly distressed and told his servant to throw both fishes back into the pond and, to the amazement of the servant, they immediately came back to life and began swimming about happily. This particular story is illustrated in a stained glass window in the parish church of St Neot in Cornwall.

It is not difficult to see that these stories are elaborations of actual events, the Glaston-bury episode recording the alteration of a door handle to suit a rather short Sacristan, and the Cornish tale perhaps the result of discovering that there were, after all, more than two fishes in the pond.

Earl Leofric eventually achieved his ambi-tion and the bones of St Neot were transferred to his priory. How this was done is the subject of legend and there are three versions of the method involved. One version of events says that Leofric sent a party of armed men down to Cornwall where they took away the body by force and brought it back to Huntingdonshire, pursued by angry Cornishmen. Another version says the earl sent an emissary to Cornwall with a large sum of money who bribed the custodian of Neot's shrine to spirit away the body by night and bring it secretly to Leofric's priory. Yet another story maintains that the transfer of the bones was achieved legally under orders signed by the king and the relevant bishops.

The truth may lie in a combination of all three stories. Even with royal sanction the transfer cannot have been popular with the Cornish people and the earl probably considered it wise to provide an armed escort for the precious relic. He may also have instructed his emissary to sweeten the custodian with money to ensure his co-operation, while removing the body at night would have been a wise move to avoid possible confrontation with objectors. What is certain is that the warden of St Neot's Cornish shrine accompanied the body on its journey, since it is on record that he was later buried in St Neots Priory.

Evidence of Anglo-Saxon occupation in the southern Eynesbury manor may be mostly buried beneath the present village buildings but a few items from the period have been found. At, or near, The Coneygeare at Eynesbury a large Anglo-Saxon cremation urn was discovered several years ago, also a number of clay loom-weights. C.F. Tebbutt held a watching brief on the area between Eynesbury Rectory and the river during the digging of foundations for the new primary school in the 1960s and identified several shallow ditches there containing sherds of Anglo-Saxon pottery.

At Eaton Socon, a dig on the site that was later occupied by a Norman castle showed that there had been Anglo-Saxon occupation before the castle was constructed and that the people who had lived there lost their homes when the castle was built. The evidence indicated the destruction of several houses, and a number of burials was found, raising the possibility of a churchyard and perhaps a church on the site. However, several of the skeletons found there bore signs of injury and, as a large number had been interred together in one grave, the likelier explanation is that the burials were the aftermath of a battle.

The village area at Eaton is known to have extended further west than the castle site. In 1961 and 1962, during the construction of Castle Hill Close, several areas of burnt daub were found, and floors indicative of a number of buildings, including one measuring 38ft. by 18ft. situated at the north-east corner of Castle Hill Close. Later investigations unearthed evidence of a possible Anglo-Saxon settlement a few hundred yards further south and west of there, and a lane running east and west to the north of the churchyard, which may have been the main village street. Iron objects of mid-to-late Saxon date were found, together with fragments of pottery dating from the ninth to the 12th centuries.

At Eaton Ford there was probably an Anglo-Saxon settlement at or near the Crosshall crossroads as an urn from the period was found there, and further south an Anglo-Saxon burial which included a sword was discovered close to the crossroads at Mill Hill.

It seems likely therefore that there were villages at all these locations, on sites which appear to have been more or less continuously occupied and re-used since prehistoric times.

Although it was a relatively peaceful region, the St Neots area did become acquainted with danger during the late 10th and early 11th centuries when Viking raiders extended their activities from the coastal lands of East Anglia to places further inland, rowing their longboats up the Ouse. The Danes, being pagans themselves, had no reservations about attacking religious houses and these were frequently their targets, since they were known to be full of gold and silver. The Vikings destroyed the abbey church at Peterborough on one raid and the monks of Leofric's priory, fearful for the safety of their precious relic, sent it to Crowland Abbey in Lincolnshire. It is not known whether the Danes ever did attempt the destruction of the first priory, but if they did so the buildings were either repaired or rebuilt, since it is recorded that the bones of St Neot had been restored to the priory by 1020. Remembering the skeletons at Eaton Socon, however, it is possible that the Anglo-Saxon community there was attacked by Vikings.

The Danes, like the Anglo-Saxons, decided that this country was a good place to live and began their own settlements. At first there was considerable animosity between the two races but after a period of sporadic warfare a truce was arranged which resulted in the Danelaw Boundary between east and west of England.

21   Castle Hill Close, Eaton Socon, at the far end of which an Anglo-Saxon village was excavated in the 1960s.

The Anglo-Saxons were required to pay a tax called Danegeld for the right to co-exist with their new neighbours, which cannot have pleased them but it did ensure comparative peace. The St Neots area was very close to the Danelaw Boundary and probably just within it but the only Scandinavian personal name to survive locally is that of Toli, the man who owned the sacred grove where the Hundred moots were held. Old field and place names which have since gone out of use sometimes reveal other links with the Danes, such as 'Scratenhoe' at Southoe which derived its name from *skratti*, a Scandinavian word for a devil or demon.

Domesday Book, compiled in 1086, gives information about ownerships during the Anglo-Saxon period and from the personal names recorded it is clear that when the Normans invaded in 1066 they met a multiracial population compounded of Celts, Angles, Saxons and Danes, known collectively as the English. At Eaton the principal manor had been held immediately before the Conquest by Ulmar, a thegn of high rank, and the manor was a soke containing two sokemen. These were men with special privileges who held estates within the manor and who, although they owed allegiance to Ulmar, could do what they liked with their land without reference to him. According to Domesday Book these sokemen were still there in 1086 but they no longer enjoyed the right to sell or grant away their land. It is this aspect of Eaton's history which resulted in it being known as Soka de Eton in 1247 and Eaton cum Soca in 1645. By the 19th century it was being called Eaton Socon. Domesday Book recorded that within the manor of Eaton there were two water mills, a church and a priest, and the river yielded 100 eels. There were 38 villager (villein) families living there, seven smallholders (bordars), who were a lower class of villager, and eight men described as 'slaves' but as the information given was relevant to 1086 the slaves may have been simply an even lower villager class. The villagers of Eaton kept 400 pigs in an area of woodland pasture and two acres of ground were used for growing vines. The manor of Sudbury was also listed in Domesday Book, where it was stated as being part of the land held by the priory of St Neot.

Eynesbury had been a royal manor before the Norman Conquest, held by King Edward. Within the manor was a church and a priest, and more watermills. There was also a sheep-fold for 662 sheep and there were 60 acres of woodland. Another small manor at Caldecote was under the lordship of Earl Tosti and this earl may also have been the tenant-in-chief representing the king in the main Eynesbury manor as that was later held by Earl Waltheof, Tosti's successor as Earl of Huntingdon, Bedford and Northampton.

The other Eynesbury manor, which later became St Neots, was held in the time of King Edward by Robert son of Wimarc. This overlord is thought to have been of partial Norman descent, although the name Wimarc sounds Anglo-Saxon. The community in Robert's manor comprised 19 villager (villein) families and five smallholders (bordars). In that manor too there was a mill and a fishery in the Ouse. The priory was listed as holding land within the manor amounting to about a quarter of its acreage and the valuation of the manor included a reference to food provision for the priory monks.

Putting all this information together, it seems that by about 1060 there was a village at Eaton Socon with a church and at least 45 houses, situated roughly where the present village is, with water mills and eel traps on the river and a patch of woodland full of pigs nearby. Modest hamlets existed elsewhere in the parish, including one at Crosshall, near the ford. On the other side of the river there were two settlements. The one to the south was roughly the same size as Eaton, with about 42 houses and a church. These villagers kept sheep rather than pigs and they too had watermills. The northern community had the priory and although it only had about 25 houses it enjoyed fishing rights in the river as well as having a mill. Moreover, the prestige of having a relic in its priory ensured that it was attracting visitors and pilgrims, bringing fame as well as revenue.

Chapter 3

Castle and Priory—1066 to 1300

William of Normandy arrived in this country in 1066 and, after defeating King Harold at Hastings, had himself crowned King William I of England. In order to bring the country under his complete control he sent out his noblemen to various parts of the kingdom with orders to erect castles at strategic sites such as river-crossings, crossroads and on high ground over-looking towns. From these castles they were to 'hold and defend' the surrounding area, under the king's patronage and authority.

One of these castles was constructed at Huntingdon, with St Neots and Eynesbury within its jurisdiction. Another was built at Bedford, its command including Eaton Socon. There may also have been a small earthwork near the river at Eaton itself, but the castle there is believed to have been built slightly later. Areas controlled by castles were described as 'baronies' and it was not until the late Norman period that Eaton was described as a 'lesser barony'.

Below the barons with their castles were the knights holding manors, and below them were tenants of farms and smallholdings within the manor, some of them freemen and others villeins or bondmen who were required to work for the lord of the manor for part of the time and could do little without his permission.

At Eynesbury the lord of the manor to the south, the Saxon Earl Waltheof, was allowed to retain his estates after the Norman Conquest because he had married Judith, the niece of William the Conqueror. In 1075, however, he rashly became involved in a revolt against the king and was promptly executed, so that by the time Domesday Book was compiled in 1086 Countess Judith was holding Eynesbury manor.

The northern manor of Eynesbury, which corresponded with what is now St Neots, was given to a member of the Norman family of de Clare. The family took its name from Clare in Suffolk where their castle and principal lands were situated, and according to Domesday Book the manor was held by 'Rohais wife of Richard son of Gilbert'. Richard himself held land at Wyboston and Sudbury, both in Bedfordshire, but they were listed as lying in the lands of St Neots Priory. There seems little doubt that the main attraction for such an important family was the priory itself, rather than the manor. The community in Rohais's manor was smaller than the one held by Countess Judith, with only half the number of dwellings and less land.

At Eaton the manor was first given to Lisois de Moutiers, a soldier, but by the time of Domesday Book it was in the hands of Eudo Dapifer, whose second name means 'steward'. As he was a steward in the royal household, a position of great prestige, this confirms Eaton as a highly valuable estate. There were links between the manors on each side of the Ouse even at that date because Eudo Dapifer's wife was the daughter of Richard de Clare, named Rohais like her mother.

It was in about 1080 that Richard and Rohais de Clare decided to rebuild the priory containing the bones of St Neot. They also wanted to remove it from the control of Ely Abbey, fill it with French monks and make it a French priory allied to the Abbey of Bec in

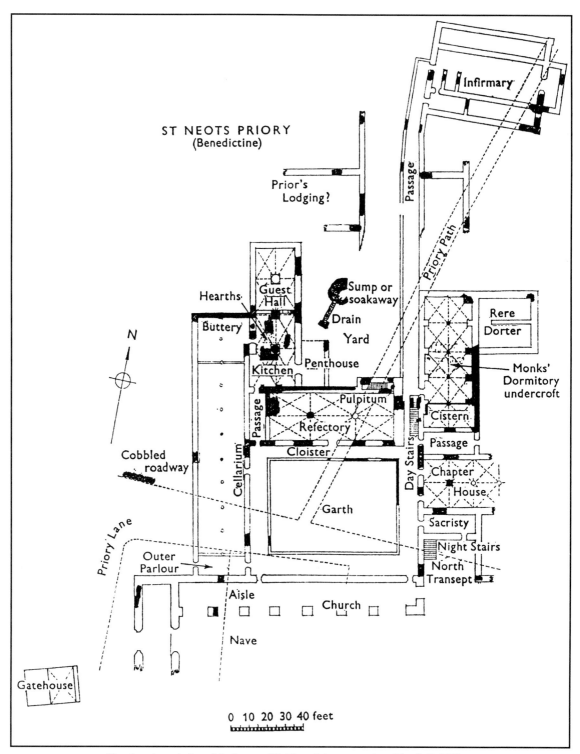

22 *A conjectural plan of the layout of St Neots Priory, as envisaged by C.F. Tebbutt.*

23 *Sketch map showing location of St Neots Priory in relation to Anglo-Saxon village site and present town.*

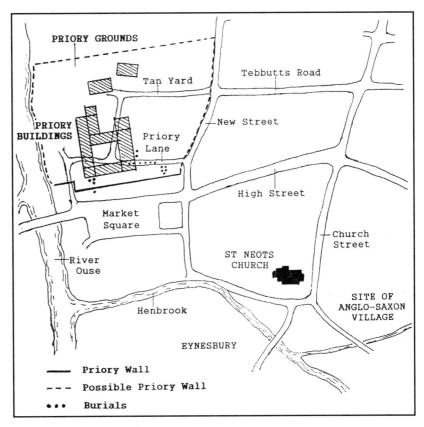

Normandy. These changes were effected over the ensuing 30 years, with the new priory being built on a site near the river. This may have been the site of the Saxon priory but the absence of evidence suggests otherwise and it was probably a completely new location.

By the time the buildings were completed Richard de Clare had died and his widow, Rohais, gave her entire manor to the priory and its monks at the re-dedication ceremony in 1113. The document which recorded the gift stated that it was given in memory of her late husband.

Details of the layout of St Neots Priory are difficult to ascertain. C.F. Tebbutt, G.T. Rudd and C. Daines conducted a number of excavations on the site in the 1960s and 1970s but their work was hampered by surrounding buildings and the results were fragmentary. Mr. Tebbutt drew up a conjectural plan of the priory based on their findings but it is not necessarily defini-

tive. It is now believed, for example, that his estimate of the position of the priory church may have been at fault. The few traces of all the buildings found were mostly in the form of robbed foundation trenches, showing ambiguous features capable of interpretation in several ways.

Contemporary documents prove that there was a church with a bell tower, a refectory where the monks ate their meals, a dormitory where they slept, a chapter house for meetings and a central cloister area. There were kitchens, a cellarium for food storage and outbuildings which included stables, storage barns, workshops and pig styes. Somewhere within the priory grounds there were the Prior's Lodging, a Guests Hall for visitors and an infirmary for the sick, and surrounding everything was a high wall, the main opening in it protected by a gatehouse and a porter's lodge.

The priory covered a wide area, extending from the edge of St Neots Common to the

24   Above. *Stone window tracery from St Neots Priory, once visible in cellar wall north of Market Square.*

25   Below left. *Spandrel from doorway of St Neots Priory, found in New Street.*

26   Below right. *Base of pillar found in situ on priory site, St Neots.*

Market Square in one direction and from the river nearly as far as New Street in the other. Evidence from the excavations suggests that only some of the buildings were entirely stone-built, others being timber-framed or timbered on a stone base. Some of the roofs were tiled, others thatched and a few were vaulted in stone.

In the area labelled by Mr. Tebbutt as the dormitory the finds included fragments of painted glass and scraps of plaster with simple painted decoration. There was also a short length of marble from a column and a piece of Barnack stone in the form of the sort of groining rib used in vaulted stone roofs, and down the centre of the building there was a line of column bases.

All this seems more suggestive of a church rather than a dormitory and the building could have been the transept of the priory church. In the area marked on Mr. Tebbutt's map as the refectory more evidence of stone vaulting was

found, together with broken glazed floor tiles, and this may have been the nave of the church. However, so many alterations to the priory buildings, and changes of use, took place in later centuries that it is impossible to be sure about the function of any of them.

A number of skeletons, unearthed in recent years, have indicated that the priory's burial ground was in the south of the site. Burials have been found in Priory Lane and on properties between there and the Market Square. The bodies were of both sexes, which suggests that the priory graveyard may have served at one time as a public burial place for the residents of the manor as well as for the monks. Some burials lay partially under the foundations of the priory wall so either the wall was moved or the interments pre-dated the priory. The most recent discoveries included one skeleton whose bones were bound by iron bands, a fact which has

27 *Excavations on the site of St Neots Priory, showing floor, walls, pillar base (top centre) and hearth, inserted later (centre).*

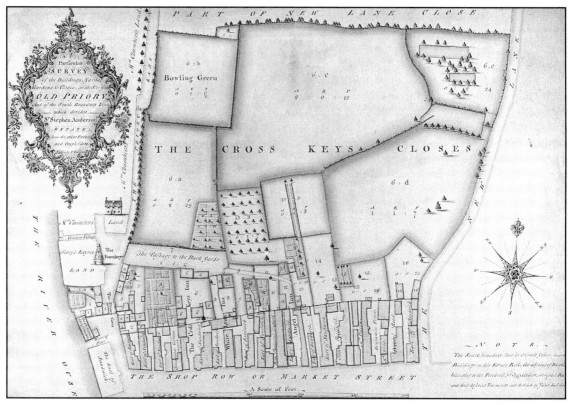

28 *Map dated 1757, showing the site formerly occupied by St Neots Priory, the priory gate and the line of the priory wall.*

raised considerable conjecture including the possibility that the bones were bound after death to secure them together and that the body could have been St Neot himself.

Unfortunately no visible trace of St Neots Priory survives. Until 1814 the gatehouse was still there and its position is marked by a stone set into the wall of a building on the west side of the lane called The Priory. It also appears in plan on a map dated 1757. The priory wall is shown as a line on the same map, running through buildings on the north side of the Market Square. According to a writer in the early years of the 19th century, the letter 'P' was inscribed on stones in each building to denote its course, since it formed a division between property formerly held by the priory and property belonging to others. The same writer also described having seen the gatehouse 'with its enormous hooks, etc., also a stone

staircase with a kind of belfry doorway and building'. The only other traces of the priory which can be seen are the pieces of stonework which still turn up from time to time during digging within the town. A few of these were set round a tree in the centre of the small car park near the library. At one time the column bases already mentioned could be seen by lifting a series of manhole covers, but they are now hidden beneath the asphalt of a supermarket car park.

The monks in St Neots Priory held an ordered life, punctuated by frequent daily services in their church. The first service was Matins at about one in the morning and the last one Compline at eight o'clock in the evening, with eight other services in between. Their meals were eaten in silence, accompanied by the reading of a religious text by one of the brothers, and any food remaining after meals was distributed to the poor at the priory gate, along with some ale and sometimes money. This distribution was known as a 'dole', which means a share, and is the origin of the slang word for unemployment benefit. The monks did very little in the way of work as all the menial tasks were performed for them by lay brothers, and their time was spent in prayer and study.

During the 12th century a small religious house was also established within the parish of Eaton Socon. A group of monks under the leadership of William of Colmworth, and not affiliated to any particular order, was given a site at Bushmead by Hugh de Beauchamp in about 1195. After the death of William in 1215 the buildings which had been erected there became an Augustinian priory. One of the

29 Above. *A 19th-century engraving of Bushmead Priory. (From G.C. Gorham's* History of St Neots, *1824.)*

30 Below. *A map showing the location of Eaton Socon Castle. (Reproduced from the 1901 Ordnance Survey map.)*

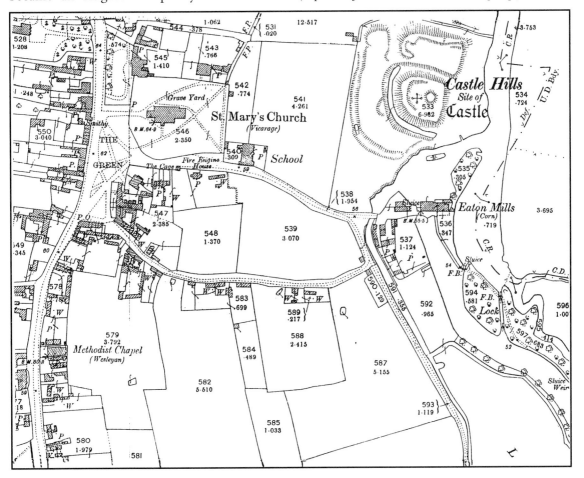

31 Earthworks on castle site at Eaton Socon, photographed in about 1900.

32 Part of a Norman arch in Eaton Socon church.

buildings survived and was restored a few years ago. Bushmead Priory was a much smaller establishment than St Neots Priory and never attained the same wealth or prestige.

Hugh de Beauchamp had acquired the manor of Eaton in about 1120 and it was probably he who built Eaton Socon castle. He was a descendant of the man, also called Hugh de Beauchamp, who held Bedford castle. From 1139 to 1153 there was civil war in England as Stephen and Matilda contested the throne. Matilda had been nominated as his successor by her father, Henry I, but several of the barons objected to the succession, partly because she was a woman and partly because they disliked her husband, Geoffrey de Plantagenet, so they invited Stephen, Henry's nephew, to become king instead. Other barons supported Matilda and warfare was inevitable. During the conflict many more castles were hastily constructed and as Eaton castle has been tentatively dated to 1140 and was never completed, it was almost certainly built during the civil war. It was of simple motte-and-bailey construction with the timber-framed living quarters within the two wards of the flat bailey area and a wooden watch-tower on the top of the conical mound which was the motte. Very few pieces of stone have been found on the site and the castle was probably never rebuilt in more substantial form but it was the construction of this castle which resulted in Eaton being described as a lesser barony, and 12th-century pottery found on the site prove that it was occupied during that period.

Matilda's son succeeded to the throne in 1154 after Stephen's death and one of his first edicts ordered the destruction of all 'adulterine' or unauthorised castles built during the civil war. This explains the fate of Eaton castle, which would have been demolished under that order, although the site may have been used for the manor house at a later date. Fragments of 13th-century pottery and traces of buildings from that era have been found on the site and 'Lady Juliana de Beauchamp' is recorded as a resident at Eaton Socon at that time.

33 *Seals used by St Neots Priory. (From G.C. Gorham's History of St Neots, 1824.)*

34 The Coneygeare, Eynesbury, location of medieval rabbit warrens.

By the time of the civil war St Neots Priory was receiving income from a weekly market. Market rights had been granted to the monks in about 1130 in a charter which allowed markets to be held every Thursday and also authorised four fairs during each year. In those days fairs were markets lasting three days which were enlivened by visiting musicians, dancers, acrobats and strolling actors.

The monks set out their market place to the south of the priory, where the market place still is, and there were soon semi-permanent stalls ranged along the southern priory wall. During excavations in 1954 C.F. Tebbutt found the remains of a small stud-and-mud lean-to building against the wall foundations which was one of these early market stalls. Tolls were paid by those using the market, providing a useful source of revenue for the priory.

Once the market got under way the next step was the building of a bridge to bring in customers from across the river. This also enabled tolls to be more easily collected from those entering the town from the west. The first bridge was entirely of timber and had no protective parapet, a fact proven by the account of an accident which occurred in 1254. The Earl of Derby, who suffered from gout, was being carried over the bridge in a sort of stretcher

when he was tipped off—whether by accident or design is unknown—by the servants carrying him. As there was no parapet he fell from the bridge, although not into the river, and suffered injuries from which he later died.

It was probably the building of the bridge which resulted in the abandonment of earlier river-crossings at The Coneygeare and Crosshall, Eaton Ford. Even though travellers had to pay a toll to use it, the bridge would have been more convenient than having to wade or row across the river. It may have been the disuse of a crossing at Crosshall which caused the odd alignment of Crosshall Road. The road from Hail Weston appears to head eastwards towards the river as if making for a crossing point but at the top of the hill it turns abruptly southwards to follow Crosshall Road to the bridge. The customers from Eaton Socon may also have forsaken a crossing further south, judging from the way in which the road from the village curves off towards the bridge.

St Neots Priory and its precious relic proved to be a great attraction to pilgrims and other visitors, and the weekly markets brought in many traders and customers. Within a fairly short period the market stalls became permanent shops and more buildings were erected along the street leading to the market place, eventually

35 Drawing of Eynesbury Hardwick stones from the chapel of St Thomas the Martyr.

linking up with the earlier settlement area at The Cross. As the name shows, this crossroads is where the Town Cross once stood, marking the area where livestock markets took place. The street is much wider at the eastern end and was known for many years as Sheep Street because on market days pens for sheep were set up there. The Town Cross was also the place where official decrees were proclaimed and in later centuries it was where the Town Crier stood to make his announcements. Fragments of the cross were found during building work on the corner of Cambridge Street and Church Street and are now preserved in the town museum.

By 1180 the nucleus of a town had grown up around the priory and, as it was under the control of the monks and their prior, it became 'St Neot's Town' and was known as St Neots from then onwards. Its inhabitants then sought permission to break away from the rest of Eynesbury to become a separate parish and when this was granted the first parish church was built. It was constructed on the same site as the present one but was undoubtedly much smaller, perhaps just a nave and chancel. The oldest masonry so far identified within the fabric of the present church is in the north wall of the chancel where stonework has been identified as late 12th-

century or early 13th-century, but two Norman stone columns were found in 1847 being used as steps between the nave of the church and the Jesus Chapel. Other remnants of the first church may lie concealed within the walls or under the flooring.

In the Eynesbury manor, which still bears the original name, the church was also rebuilt by the new Norman overlord. The surviving 12th-century stonework there is also part of the chancel walls and there are Norman columns separating the nave from the north aisle. Eynesbury parish is a straggling one and it must have been difficult for parishioners living in the south and east to attend church regularly, so two chapels-of-ease were built for their convenience. One was at Weald, where it served the village and two hamlets at Upper and Lower Wintringham. Its foundations were excavated several years ago close to an area marked 'Chapel Yard' on a map dated 1902. At Eynesbury Hardwick in the south there was a chapel dedicated to St Thomas the Martyr. Pieces of Norman masonry from this building could still be seen up until a few years ago, lying around the site once occupied by a moated manor house and later by a farmhouse. Its chaplain was a monk from St Neots Priory.

Very little has been found locally to show the domestic architecture of the Norman period, but one 12th-century building was discovered at Skin Yard, Eynesbury. It measured 14ft. by 9ft. 6in. and had walls made of clay. Inside was a clay shelf running round two of the walls at the base, which perhaps acted as rudimentary seating, although this had been covered by a floor added later. Bones of pigs and sheep and pieces of 12th-century pottery were scattered on the earth floor and the doorway was set with cobbles.

Eaton Socon parish church was also rebuilt under the Normans. One theory is that the original Saxon church was destroyed when the castle was constructed, but that has not so far been verified, although several buildings were certainly knocked down in the process of castle-building. The Norman church was undoubtedly on the same site as the present one. Two relics of it can be seen in the present church. One is the font, a square stone one with blind arcading decoration, and the other is part of a semi-circular arch, decorated with carved chevrons.

The dominant force in the region during the 12th and 13th centuries was St Neots Priory, and it was also the wealthiest. Local landholders gave the monks several large acreages of land and left money to the priory in their Wills. Churches in a number of counties contributed tithes and other fees and there were generous donations from travellers being accommodated in the Guests Hall and pilgrims paying their respects to the bones of St Neot. As lords of the manor the monks received rents, fees and gifts from their tenants and the services of villeins (villagers) to farm their land. They also made money from market tolls, which became more and more lucrative as time progressed. So much of the Prior's time was occupied in manorial duties that a Town Bailiff had to be employed to collect rents and a Market Bailiff to collect tolls.

As well as wealth, the priory had great prestige and was visited by many noblemen, bishops and others of high rank including royalty. Henry II visited St Neots in 1156,

where he would have been entertained in the Prior's Lodging, his retinue of several hundred knights and servants being accommodated in the Guests Hall and elsewhere. Henry III also visited the priory, staying there in 1229, 1235 and 1236.

The town prospered along with the priory. Documents from the period refer to goldsmiths and metal workers resident in the town who would have been making religious mementoes including pilgrim badges, since even in those days travellers liked to take home souvenirs to show where they had been.

In 1279 the Hundred Rolls were compiled, which were a record of holdings similar to Domesday Book, but more detailed with manors and their tenants listed under each Hundred. Unfortunately the entries have not all survived and there are none for either St Neots or Eaton Socon, but the Eynesbury details are very informative.

At that time the manor was held jointly by Margaret, Countess de Ferrers, and her sister Elena la Zouche, heirs of the Earl of Winchester. Together they held 553 acres of arable land, nine and a half acres of meadow and 15 acres of pasture. The women also held the right of presentation to Eynesbury church, 'certain fisheries in the water which is called Use' and right of warrenage. Warrenage was the right to keep rabbits, for eating not as pets, and the Eynesbury warrens were situated at The Coneygeare where large earth mounds were raised in which the animals bred and multiplied, with a warrener in charge to keep the 'coneys' within the warren fence, and the villagers out.

The villein tenants of the manor were required to work for part of each week on the land held by the sisters as their demesne. This was a condition of their tenancy of their own land and the terms were set out in the Hundred Rolls.

Reginald Balle, villein, holds half a virgate of land which contains 18 acres for the underwritten customary duties, namely working every week for two days, that is on Monday and Wednesday up to noon at the will of the Lady and, if he has a plough for arable work, every Friday up to noon or at the will of the Lady. And he mows one rood of meadow at the time of mowing. And when he mows in the great meadow with his fellow villeins he has one pightle of pasture and he mows for the whole day; and he gives two hens a year ... If he dies his wife or son will hold the land for the same customary duties without paying fine or heriot.

Countess Margaret had 17 other villeins holding their land on the same conditions, and her sister Elena had eight villeins. Both women also had tenants described as 'cottars' holding cottages and very small amounts of land in return for light duties or money rent, and these were probably widows or villein men too old and infirm to work.

There were a number of free tenants within the manor too. The tenant-in-chief, who acted as lord of the manor since the two sisters are unlikely to have lived at Eynesbury, was Thomas de Berkley. He held a large estate and had 31 villein tenants and nine free tenants of his own. Margaret and Elena had 27 free tenants in addition to Thomas de Berkley, some paying a nominal money rent and others paying a token rent or rent in kind. One of Margaret's free tenants paid her a pair of white gloves once a year and another paid with five fowls. A third tenant had to supply two spurs worth twopence, and other tenants within the manor paid with various amounts of pepper. Eleven tenants, although renting their holdings from the Countess, paid their money directly to the Chapel of St Thomas the Martyr at Eynesbury Hardwick.

This was a period when surnames were being formed to differentiate between men with the same Christian names. They described relationship, such as 'Stephen son of John' which became Johnson; place of residence or origin such as 'Peter ad Pontem'—Peter at the bridge—and 'Thomas de Paxton'; a personal characteristic such as 'John le Long', or an occupation. The latter category shows the occupations of some of Eynesbury's residents. Walter le Carpenter is easily identifiable but some names were Latinised. Robert Faber was the local smith, for example, and William Pistore was a miller. Henry le Brazur probably worked in metal and Henry Blichere perhaps with cloth. The location

names used as surnames show that tenants had come from as far away as Daventry, Sheffield and Somerset.

There were 84 dwellings mentioned or implied in the entries as being in the village of Eynesbury, with another 15 dwellings at Eynesbury Hardwick in addition to the manor house and chapel. Caldecote also had several dwellings but the number was not specified.

Both Eaton Socon and St Neots were busy places in the early Middle Ages because of the main roads passing through them. The Great North Road also passed through the village of Sudbury at the Crosshall crossroads and it witnessed several cases of highway crime, two of which were recorded in the 1260s.

In 1265 two women and the son of one of them 'were on their way from the market at St Neots to the Leper Hospital at Sudbury' when they were attacked by a local gang of two men and two women who attempted to rob them. In those days there was no police force so 'the hue was raised' and all able-bodied men within earshot were required to come to the victims' aid. One of those who came to help was William the Shepherd of Sudbury, who died as a result. On Hail Bridge between Sudbury and Southoe one of the robbers 'struck William the shepherd with a sword on the right side of his head and cut away part of his head with the brains and the right ear, so that he died forthwith ...'. The rest of the men from Sudbury managed to arrest the killer and the two women accomplices but the fourth robber fled to Diddington church and claimed Sanctuary. This crime took place at twilight, or in the original Latin 'inter canem et lupem' meaning 'between dog and fox'.

The leper hospital referred to in the account was probably looked after by monks from St Neots Priory and would have been well away from Sudbury village as leprosy was a disease very much feared by the people. Other documents show that Sudbury also had a hermitage where a solitary monk lived, supported by the lord of the manor and various bequests from local noblemen.

36   The ridge-and-furrow of Sudbury's arable fields at Crosshall, Eaton Ford, revealed by snow.

Two years after the episode at Hail Bridge another murder took place just outside Sudbury. The right of Sanctuary mentioned in the first account was an interesting custom. Any felon or wrongdoer, or an escaping prisoner, could claim 40 days of respite from retribution by getting himself into a church, or in some cases simply into a churchyard. Once there he had to decide whether to stand trial or choose voluntary exile from the country. Since the dungeons of the time were horrific places in which many people died before their trials were arranged, most offenders chose exile. This choice involved walking to a given port of embarkation, bare-footed, wearing a coarse cotton shift and carrying a wooden cross, a journey which had to be completed within the 40 days of Sanctuary. As long as the offender kept to main roads he was supposed to be allowed to pass unmolested but this was not always the case.

In 1267 'a certain unknown man' had escaped imprisonment at Southoe and had gained Sanctuary in Southoe church. Choosing exile, he set off from Southoe along the Great North Road en route for Dover, but he was ambushed by four men from Hail Weston who 'assaulted him with swords and wounded him in the heart so that he fell at once; and later in the King's Highway outside Sudbury they cut off his head with an axe'. The motive of these attackers can hardly have been robbery in view of what the traveller was wearing and the likeliest explanation is that they were victims of the crime for which the man had been imprisoned and they were exacting their revenge.

Life was obviously hazardous at times for those living in the region of St Neots during the 13th century, but it was exciting and colourful too. There were fairs and markets and a constant flow of visitors bringing news and gossip from far and wide. Now and then there was even a royal visit to break the monotony of working in the fields.

Chapter 4

Disaster and Dissolution—1300 to 1600

The manor of Sudbury at Eaton Ford was held in the early years of the 14th century by John, son of William de Sudbury. He seems to have been somewhat wild by nature, unlike his father. In 1315 he was twice imprisoned for trespass and in 1316 he was convicted of robbery. He apparently redeemed himself by serving with Edward II during his campaign against the Scots in 1322 and he was summoned to represent Eaton in parliament and council in 1322 and 1324.

When he died in 1333 the Sudbury manor was described as consisting of a manor house, a 'broken-down dovecote', 200 acres of arable land, six acres of meadow, 20 acres of woodland and an island in the Ouse from which reeds were supplied to St Neots Priory. John had been receiving rents from his tenants amounting to 36s. and three pounds of pepper. There was no mention of either leper hospital or hermitage in the Inquisition Post Mortem and the manor may have been in decline by then, which was not surprising if its overlord spent much of his time in prison or away on military or political business. After the 17th century the manor of Sudbury did not appear in records, although the name 'Sudbury Meadow' survived until the 19th century, and the ridge and furrow of the village's arable fields can be seen as grassy waves on a golf course at the top of the hill. Sudbury's manor house or hall was at the crossroads, hence the name Crosshall Road.

St Neots, Eynesbury and Eaton Socon all had their open fields, meadows and commons as well, surrounding the houses and extending to the parish boundaries. The large acreages of arable land in the open fields were held in dispersed strips by the tenants, who were also entitled to a strip of meadow grass for hay and the right to turn their livestock out onto the common grazing areas. Farming took place on a communal basis and there had to be mutual agreement on the dates when ploughing, harvesting or haymaking was to take place. Grazing, as well as being available on the commons, was also permitted on the arable after harvesting and on the meadows after the hay had been made. Haymaking had to be complete by 1 August, which was Lammas, hence the name Lammas Meadow at St Neots.

The rules which regulated all this were agreed at yearly meetings of the manor court. The earliest court records for St Neots date from the mid–16th century, but the conditions recorded in them had probably applied for many years. One law stated 'that no man shall put any horses, cows or other cattle into the meadow before the hay be carried away, on pain of 6s. 8d.' Another rule decreed 'that no Artificer shall keep on the commons more than one horse or two kye ... that no Artificer shall keep above four hogs upon the commons ...' and that 'every man shall ring his hogs before Martinmas next ...'.

Special allowances were made for the local butchers who, in the absence of refrigeration, had to keep their meat on the hoof until required. The court rolls revealed that 'no butcher shall put into the Illands Common above

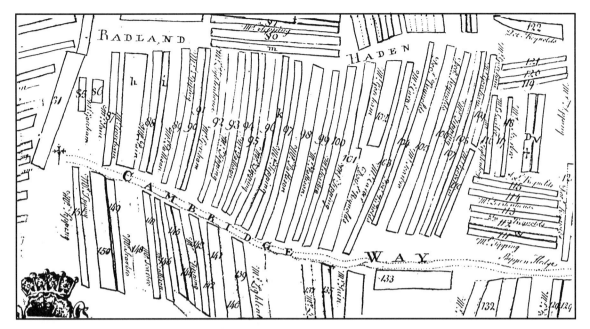

37 *Part of an 18th-century map of St Neots open fields showing strips of arable land to north and south of Cambridge Street.*

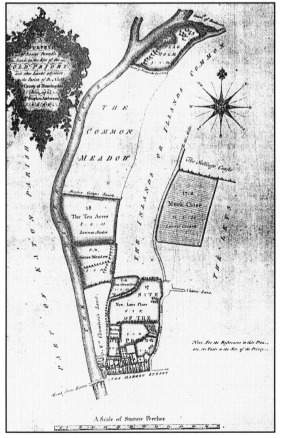

38 *Map dated 1757 showing the Islands or 'Illands Common'.*

the number of 13 sheep at once, and those not before Lammas, and so many not above one week together.' Other regulations ensured that only residents of St Neots used the grazing facilities and that all tenants attended the allocation of meadow strips or were fined 8d. Paupers were permitted to glean what crops remained after harvesting.

In 1338 England embarked on the Hundred Years War against France, a conflict which spluttered on intermittently and had a disastrous effect on St Neots Priory. Because the priory was full of French monks and was a cell of the Abbey of Bec in France it was declared to be an 'alien priory'. The king demanded an annual fee from the monks which amounted to over half their normal annual income and in addition the priory was ostracised by travellers and pilgrims, cutting off another valuable source of revenue. At one stage the monks were even accused of spying for the French and were removed from St Neots to Turvey in Bedfordshire. Fortunately common sense prevailed and they were allowed to return to the priory.

Adding to the priory's other problems was the Black Death. In 1348 this epidemic of bubonic plague is believed to have killed off about a third of the total population of this country and, as it was highly contagious, it spread rapidly in communal groups such as those in a monastery. There are no records to show how many monks died from the disease at St Neots Priory but an entry for 1350 in the priory's cartulary referred to the scarcity of servants owing to the plague. At Eaton Socon church a priest died and Richard, the Prior of Bushmead, also succumbed. Doubtless many ordinary townspeople and villagers in all the local communities suffered similar fates. It is now known that the Black Death was not necessarily to blame for the disappearance of some medieval villages, but it was probably a contributing factor and may have been the final nail in the coffin of the village and manor of Sudbury. Other villages and hamlets which may have begun their decline with the loss of population which occurred at this time are Upper and Lower Wintringham,

Weald, Caldecote and Eynesbury Hardwick to the east of the river, and Begwary, Basmead and Bushmead to the west.

One of the other effects of the Black Death and the sudden drop in population was the break-up of the feudal system. Men who had been bound to the manor in villeinage were able to benefit from the shortage of labour and buy or negotiate their freedom from bondage. Freemen were able to move from place to place in search of better wages, or to buy and sell land, so the social structure of the country began to change.

Another outcome of the labour shortage was the change of use of some of the land. What had for centuries been arable was turned into grazing land for livestock, particularly sheep, which required fewer men to cope with. This is what seems to have happened at St Neots. Throughout the 13th century, priory documents referred to acreages of arable in 'Inland' and 'Little-Inland' as part of the open fields, the names denoting areas close to the town. After 1350 there were no similar references and by the 16th century 'Illands Common' appeared in documents. An 18th-century map makes the progression clear by labelling the area 'The Inlands or Illands Common' and its present name of Islands Common is a corruption. This large grazing area joined others which were in use at that time, including Hawkesden Leys at the top of Priory Hill which is still a common.

A Valuation of St Neots Priory dated 1370 shows that the monks were then receiving rents from their properties and fees from the markets but their finances were still evidently at a low level as they had been unable to repair three watermills which had been destroyed by a severe flood. Life was obviously very difficult for the inmates of the priory and in 1378 three French monks were given permission to return to France. This left only three others remaining apart from the prior and when he died in 1404 an English prior was appointed in his place. English monks were then recruited and the prior applied for the right to sever connections with Bec and become an English priory in 1409, a request which was granted.

39 *Islands Common, St Neots from the south.*

40 *Hawkesden Leys Common in about 1910 when golf was played there.*

The previous hard years had naturally taken their toll and this was revealed in the reports of the Bishop's Visitations in 1432 and 1439. All the priory buildings were said to be in need of repair and there were gaps in the perimeter wall which allowed anyone from the town to wander in and out of the priory at will. The bell tower, which had fallen down many years before, had not been rebuilt and there were no seats in the cloisters. The priory church was in a poor state too, one of the monks complaining that when it rained the brothers dared not open their books for fear of getting them wet! The bishop recorded that there was no proper Guests Hall for visitors so all kinds of secular people were eating with the monks in their refectory, and the vow of silence was not being kept. There had been a Guests Hall at the priory throughout the 13th century and it was probably the lack of visitors during the 'alien priory' period which caused the monks to stop using it and perhaps give it another function. One theory is that it stood on the site later occupied by *The Cross Keys* inn on the Market Square. Crossed keys are a symbol of St Peter's in Rome, and of the Pope, so buildings which served a religious purpose were often marked with this symbol. A Guests Hall marked by crossed keys could have been converted into an inn in the 14th century leaving the priory with nowhere to accommodate visitors.

Even worse than the structural disintegration reported in the Visitations was the disintegration of morals and discipline among the priory monks. The prior accused the brothers of being too sleepy to get up for Matins in the morning and he complained that they did not keep silence in church but 'chatter therein with secular folk as though they were at market'. The monks themselves, interviewed individually, accused the sub-prior of being 'to some degree out of his wits and yet he is suffered to remain in office' but they reserved their strongest criticism for the prior. They said that he spent so much time on town and manorial business that he neglected services and failed to keep proper accounts. He was also accused of having bribed his way into office and—worst of all—to have 'a very suspect reputation with a married woman from Hardwick named Agnes Actone'.

The prior and Agnes were summoned before the bishop and the prior admitted the bribery, for which he was apparently pardoned because he remained in office. Both he and Agnes denied any misbehaviour but nevertheless promised not to do it again! There was a severe rebuke regarding the other failings and this seems to have had the desired effect as by 1507 the buildings had been repaired and discipline had been restored.

A new Guests Hall had been provided by then as it was referred to under its alternative name of 'hospice' in accounts dated 1505. In 1471 a document had mentioned 'a hospice called the Bulle' which suggests that the monks, instead of building a new Guests Hall, had rented a building on the Market Square. *The Bull Inn* once stood on the site later occupied by Paine & Company and the name survived until the 1970s as the title of a small bar on their premises. Just as the crossed keys signified a building used by a religious house, a papal seal or 'bulla' had a similar purpose and may have given rise to the name of the inn.

It was during the 15th century that St Neots and Eaton Socon rebuilt their parish churches. This would have involved working in stages, since part of the buildings would have had to

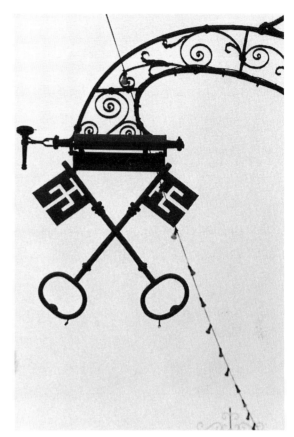

41 The inn sign of The Cross Keys *in Market Square, St Neots.*

remain in use during alterations. At St Neots it was probably the chancel which was used, since that was merely modified by being lengthened and given a new roof and windows. The rest of the church was completely rebuilt, with side aisles to the nave, chapels each side of the chancel and a south porch. The chapels were used by local guilds, groups of people in the same trade or profession, or groups banding together for some religious or social reason. In some medieval churches a chapel was endowed by a local family as their own private place of worship with its own priest, as at Eaton Socon where a chantry was established by Ralph de Beauchamp in 1291. None of the local churches are recorded as having had trade guilds but there was a Guild of Corpus Christi at Eaton Socon and a Guild of Jesus at St Neots.

The last part of St Neots church to be built was the splendid tower, rising 130ft. above the town and a landmark for the surrounding area. The interior of the church was fitted out in a suitably impressive fashion too, the interior roof timbers being carved with a variety of creatures, real and imaginary, and originally painted and gilded. There was a great deal of colour throughout with stained glass windows, scraps of which are preserved in the church, and wall paintings. Although they are no longer coloured, the carved roof timbers are still in place and were recently restored. When it was first built the church was also provided with carved benches but these were replaced in the 19th century. Above the chancel screen a rood loft carried a crucifixion and statues of saints and was reached by a stone staircase set into the chancel arch.

42 Left. *A 19th-century drawing of St Neots church, with pathways now disused.*

43 Below. *Eaton Socon church as it was before being burnt down in 1930.*

44 Above. *The interior of Eaton Socon church before the fire, showing the carved 15th-century benches.*

45 Right. *Two of the 15th-century carved bench-ends in the north aisle of Eynesbury church.*

At Eaton Socon the church was rebuilt in similar style, with a fine tower almost the equal of the one at St Neots. There may not have been so much money to spend at Eaton, judging from the fact that some stonework from a previous building was used, including a doorway, but no expense was spared on the interior. Until the fire of 1930 destroyed them a fine collection of benches with carved poppyheads filled the church and there was also a carved screen. Accounts of the church as it used to be describe it in glowing terms, using words such as 'beautiful' and 'very elegant'.

Eynesbury church had been extensively rebuilt during the 13th century and the only alterations carried out in the 15th century were the addition of a clerestorey to the nave, providing light to the side aisles, and the provision of new benches. Some of these benches survive, decorated with stiffly carved leaves and various beasts

46 *No. 42 High Street, St Neots, a restored 15th-century building, once a merchant's house.*

47 *The Chequers, St Mary's Street, Eynesbury, probably medieval with later additions.*

48 *The 15th-century* Nags Head *in Berkley Street, Eynesbury, demolished when the present public house was built.*

49   The Plough, *Eaton Socon, in the 1930s.*

50   A view of Eaton Socon from The Green. The medieval house can be seen on the right in the middle distance.

51   Cottages in Huntingdon Street, St Neots, now demolished. In one of them a medieval door was discovered.

including deer, goats and chickens, once known colloquially as 'Eynesbury Zoo'. Judging from old photographs of the bench-ends at Eaton Socon, they may well have been carved by the same local craftsman.

Very few secular buildings have survived from the 15th century, at least visibly, although structures from that period may be hidden behind frontages which were added later. Until comparatively recently, for example, a fine timber-framed building erected in the 15th century lay concealed behind brickwork on the corner of Church Walk in St Neots. Once discovered it was carefully restored and now provides a welcome touch of character to the High Street. It is believed to have been built for a wealthy merchant, perhaps one dealing in corn, as the carvings which run along its bressummer are thought to represent sheaves of wheat.

Also dating from the same period is the *Old Falcon* on St Neots Market Square, its frontage concealing a much older interior. It may have started as an inn or alehouse like several others which were round the square at that time. An inn called *The Antelope* was recorded in 1542 and *The Bull*, as already mentioned, was there in 1471. In other parts of the town there would have been more hostelries to accommodate the constant flow of travellers which passed through the town.

Eynesbury's oldest surviving secular medieval building is *The Chequers* in St Mary's Street. Although roughly dated to the early 16th century it is likely to have been there a century earlier. During the Middle Ages, when there were no banks, innkeepers acted as money-changers and money-lenders and they advertised the fact by displaying a 'chequer-board', a device marked out in squares, on which transactions were calculated. It is from the use of such a board that the Chancellor of the Exchequer derives his title, and it may be the derivation of the name of the Eynesbury inn. In Berkley Street there was once also another 15th-century building under the sign of *The Nags Head* but it was demolished to make room for the present public house.

At Eaton Socon the buildings which have the longest history are also probably the inns, although these are so much altered that it is difficult to tell. *The White Horse* and *The Plough* both claimed extreme age at one time, the latter bearing the extravagant boast that it was 11th-century! *The Plough*, now no longer an inn, appears to be the older building but there may be medieval timbers behind the 18th-century frontage of *The White Horse* as well. Until a few years ago one genuinely medieval building stood on the main road at Eaton Socon, near the corner of Nelson Road. It was built in typical style with a central hall and cross wings and had steeply pitched and gable-ended roofs above timber-framed walls. It was in a very poor state by the 1960s and, as no-one seemed able or willing to repair it in situ, it was sold, dismantled and re-erected in another village several miles away.

During the first few years of the 16th century St Neots and its priory enjoyed a period of mutual prosperity. An account of priory finances for 1505 shows how closely interwoven were the lives of monks and townspeople. Many laymen, and a few women too, were employed by the priory, some within its walls and others in the town or on the farms. There were bakers, brewers, cooks, carters and labourers and among other employees there was a barber, a tailor, a washerwoman, an organist and a man to help with the choir. Guests in the hospice were being treated well, judging from the animals recorded as having been slaughtered for food there. A hundred sheep were killed and an unspecified number of bullocks, cows and calves yielding 38 stones of tallow as a by-product. Nor did the monks starve themselves either. Among income received was money for the hides of 26 bullocks and seven calves.

The priory received rent from houses and shops in 'Market Strete, Saynte Maristrete, Cambrigestrete, Huntyngdonstrete, Neystrete' and some parts of Eynesbury. St Mary's Street at that time was the name for Church Street and 'Neystrete' was perhaps New Street. As well as these rents there was other revenue from four watermills, a horse-mill, a dovecote

52   Engravings of some of the door panels from Priory House. (From G.C. Gorham's History of St Neots *1824.)*

and a bakehouse, all of which were rented out to townspeople, and there were tolls from markets and fairs. More money was donated to the priory by pilgrims coming to see the bones of St Neot. According to Gorham's history, Leland visited the priory in 1538 and saw two other relics there. One was a vest believed to have been worn by the saint, 'made of hair cloth in the Irish manner' and the other was St Neot's comb, 'made of a little bone of two fingers' breadth, into which was inserted small fishes' teeth.'

The prosperous period for the priory came to an abrupt end, however, in the 1530s. Henry VIII, who had come to the throne in 1509, quarrelled with the Pope in 1529 and broke away from the Catholic Church to establish the Church of England with himself as its head. In a series of Acts a few years later he set about the Dissolution of the Monasteries. Abbeys, priories and other religious institutions

set up under Catholicism were forced to surrender to the king all their premises and possessions, and the monks and nuns were pensioned off and evicted. The assets of these establishments were then appropriated by the king or given to his family and friends, or sold to swell the royal finances.

St Neots Priory surrendered in 1534 and the 12 monks who were then in residence were given pensions of between £5 and £8 a year, apart from the prior, John Raunds, who received £40. When Bushmead Priory surrendered, its prior, Richard Burre, was awarded a more modest pension of £12, and the chaplain of the chapel of St Thomas the Martyr at Eynesbury Hardwick only received £3 a year.

In 1542 part of the priory's possessions, including the priory buildings and farms at Wintringham and Monks Hardwick, were sold to Sir Richard Williams, also known as

Cromwell. The rest of the estate, including the lordship of the manor of St Neots, was given by Henry to his daughter Elizabeth, who later became Queen Elizabeth I.

Sir Richard appears to have fitted into the local community without any problems but his son Francis, who succeeded him, was a different character who was constantly in dispute with other townspeople. All the tenants of the manor were entitled to graze their animals on the commons but Sir Francis Williams tried to exclude them from several areas which he claimed were his alone and not held in common. The constant bickering eventually went to official arbitration and the Award which recorded the outcome shows that—as might be expected—Sir Francis came off best. Although Islands Common and Hawkesden Leys were secured as grazing for all, he succeeded in acquiring exclusive use of several other areas of former common land. The Arbitration Award of 1564 is interesting in many ways as it reveals that there was once a right of way for towns-people through the priory grounds to Islands Common whenever a fair took place there, and that the holders of common rights could keep a common bull for breeding.

Bushmead Priory and its holdings passed initially to the St John family of Bletsoe in Bedfordshire but were exchanged by them shortly afterwards for other property and became the possession of Sir William Gascoigne. Even he did not hold it for long and William Gery was in possession by 1553.

The removal of all the religious houses caused difficulties for the parish churches. Without the commitment of the monks and nuns to provide for the sick and the poor, the burden of welfare fell upon the churches and their churchwardens. The break-up of the feudal system had increased the number of paupers as tenants were no longer able to rely upon the paternalistic care of an overlord, who would have looked after the widows and orphans of his villeins. Local benefactors did their best to supplement the relief being paid out by church-wardens, but eventually a system was introduced

under which all those able to do so had to contribute money. In 1591, 67 villagers at Eaton Socon, out of a population of 879, were paying rates to support 25 paupers, mostly widows. Payments levied were between one penny and eight pence, one man paying his penny in three instalments! In 1596 an Eaton woman was paid twopence a week to teach the paupers' children to make lace, an early example of the lace schools which were a common feature in later centuries. Similar measures were undoubtedly being taken at Eynesbury and St Neots although records for those areas do not survive.

The first school in the town of St Neots was established during the 16th century, although the priory had supported schools for boys destined for a monastic life since 1260. The prior of Bushmead had also applied for a licence to start a school in 1332 but his death from plague had caused the project to be abandoned. By 1556, however, the town of St Neots had a school because in that year a man called Faucet was described as a priest and schoolmaster. This school's pupils were exclusively the sons of clergy and gentry, two of them being the sons of the Vicar of St Neots. This establishment, which held its classes in the parish church, was referred to as 'St Neots Grammar School' in the 16th century and its master is believed to have occupied the 15th-century building on the corner of Church Walk.

In the years which followed the Dissolution of the Monasteries the buildings of St Neots Priory and Bushmead Priory gradually disappeared, although at Bushmead one building survived and was restored a few years ago by English Heritage. Nothing remains above ground of St Neots Priory apart from the scraps of stonework previously mentioned. For several years a house on the priory site contained an old door composed of panels believed to have come from the priory church, but this door was later sold and its present whereabouts is unknown. The carvings on the door panels depicted St Michael holding scales, St George, St Matthew and a young nobleman with a sword. Other pieces of carving showed scraps of foliage and mouldings. These carvings were drawn (rather badly) in Gorham's history, and a faint photograph of them also exists, but without the originals it is impossible to say if they are likely to have come from the priory. By 1584, when a lease was drawn up regarding the former priory's mill and brewhouse by the bridge, the buildings concerned were 'in great decay and ruin' and the priory itself was probably in a similar state. Most of the stone-work was sold off as valuable building material or put to other uses. A local tradition says that some of it was used to build St Neots Bridge, which may be true of the bridge which was constructed in 1588.

It was in that year that the counties of Bedfordshire and Huntingdonshire decided to rebuild the bridge. Both counties had to be involved because the river formed the boundary between them, and a joint body decided on its design and shared the costs. The new bridge was to be 704ft. in length and 7½ft. in width. On the Eaton side, where a causeway was required, the 43 arches would be entirely of timber but where the bridge crossed the water the 29 timber arches would be supported by stone piers. These piers would be six feet high to bring them as high as the river rose when in flood and so protect the timbers from rotting. It is possible that stone from the priory buildings was used for these piers, the other materials required being 153 tons of timber and unspecified quantities of sand and lime. It is to be hoped that the bridge was completed by 1591 as in that year the town suffered such a severe flood that swans were seen swimming in the market place.

No-one knows what happened to the bones of St Neot after the Dissolution. They may have been seized and destroyed by Henry's commissioners who were ordered to remove all relics and other 'superstitious' items from religious houses, or the bones could have been spirited away by devout monks. One local legend maintains that the saint's body was buried at Southoe, but the truth is that we shall never know its eventual fate.

Chapter 5

Civil War, Commonwealth and Restoration—1600 to 1700

Queen Elizabeth died in 1603 and was succeeded by James I. In 1620 he granted the lordship of the manor of St Neots to Sir Richard Lucy, who sold it a few years later to Sir Sidney Montague, a member of the family which became Earls of Sandwich and Earls of Manchester. The Earls of Sandwich held the lordship throughout the two centuries which followed and, as they lived at Hinchingbrooke near Huntingdon, their affairs in St Neots were managed by a bailiff. Robert Payne had served as Royal Bailiff to Elizabeth from 1566 and he continued to act in that capacity for the Montagues, his son Edward succeeding him in the office in 1667.

53-54   A drawing of a 17th-century plaster panel in the wall of a building at the foot of St Neots bridge. Originally the building was a butcher's shop, seen here in 1863, and then became the Half Moon *inn and then the* Bridge Hotel.

When the old St Neots bridge was demolished in the 1960s it was found to have the date 1617 inscribed on one of its stones, which may indicate that it was built in that year, replacing the previous stone-and-timber structure with one entirely of stone. The bridge was certainly rebuilt at some time during the 17th century but there is no evidence to prove exactly when. The earliest representation of the bridge, a drawing believed to have been made early in the 18th century, shows a very simple construction without the fancy embellishments which appear in later pictures and this may have been what the 17th-century bridge looked like. A reproduction of this picture appears in Tebbutt's *St Neots*.

Improvements to bridges, and to the river itself, were very much the concern of local people at the time, as transporting goods by

55   Old cottages, 17th-century or older, on the Great North Road, Eaton Socon. Those on the right have since been demolished.

56   A view of the River Ouse at Little Paxton, with the Haling Way on the left.

water was easier than moving them by road. The condition of the roads made travel of any kind a long and difficult process, both for travellers on horseback or in unsprung coaches and for carters of goods in waggons drawn by heavy horses. In winter they found themselves bogged down in mud and in summer the ruts baked hard, causing numerous upsets. The authorities in each parish were responsible for keeping the roads within their boundaries in repair, a task which was a serious problem for small parishes which had major roads passing through them. As Macaulay wrote, 'It was not in the power of the parishes in Huntingdonshire to mend a highway worn by the constant traffic between the West Riding of Yorkshire and London.' He was referring at the time to the Old North Road to the east, but there were similar problems along the Great North Road which ran through Eaton Socon. A petition to parliament in 1666 resulted in the first turn-pikes being set up in an effort to exact tolls from road-users which would help to defray the cost of road repairs, and by the end of the century there were bars across many roads which could be turned aside on payment of a toll.

Meanwhile improvements to river navigation had also been taking place. In about 1615 sluices were constructed between St Neots and St Ives, enabling boats to pass more easily between the two towns, the right to levy tolls on goods transported being acquired by John Jackson of St Neots in 1626. A few years later Arnold Spencer obtained a patent to make the river navigable as far as Bedford and he began by building a sluice at Eaton Socon. He also scoured the river as far as Great Barford and later gained control of the stretch of river between St Neots and St Ives. Boats were initially hauled along the river by men walking along a towpath called the Haling Way, but their labours were later taken over by horses. The old haling or hauling way survives as part of a long distance footpath and one of the streets in Little Paxton is named after it, although it is incorrectly spelt as 'Hayling Way'.

57 *An illustration from the Civil War pamphlet.*

58   The statue of Oliver Cromwell in the Market Place at St Ives.

Easier travel and transport by road and river was good for trade in the town but the period of comparative prosperity which resulted was a brief one. In 1625 Charles I became king and was in conflict with his parliament almost from his accession. He was a wilful, autocratic man, over-ruling the members of parliament, and even dismissing them entirely on one occasion, in order to get his own way. Those members who were also at court sided with Charles and those who were not took the side of parliament and it became a struggle for power between two groups of the aristocracy. As head of the Church of England Charles I also faced the problems of a growing trend away from the established church and towards Puritanism, and the survival of Catholicism, both of which also challenged his authority.

In 1641 all males over the age of 16 were required to sign a document affirming their allegiance to the Protestant Church and, by inference, to the king himself. Needless to say, the majority of men felt it expedient to sign, whatever their religious leanings, and there are no records of dissent at St Neots or Eynesbury. At Diddington, however, two brave souls refused to sign and were listed as 'Popish recusants'.

The Protestation Returns list 278 males at St Neots and 133 at Eynesbury. Assuming that there were at least as many females and roughly as many children under the age of 16, there was probably a population of about 900 at St Neots and 400 at Eynesbury. The Protestation Returns for Eaton Socon are missing so it is not possible to estimate the population there.

The quarrels between king and parliament culminated inevitably in the Civil War which began in 1642. Loyalties were divided locally and there was support for both sides. Sir Edward Montague, Earl of Manchester, supported Parliament and became an important officer in the Roundhead Army, but his uncle, who was lord of the manor of St Neots, was a Royalist who had several times entertained the king at Hinchingbrooke and he supported Charles. Sir James Beverley of Eaton Socon was for Parliament but the Gery family of Bushmead were Royalists. William Gery fought in the Royalist Army and was taken prisoner at the surrender of Colchester in 1648 and his brother George was captured at Naseby in 1646. The sums of money required to ransom them severely depleted the value of the Bushmead estate.

The ordinary townspeople and villagers of the local area probably differed in their loyalties too, but if there were supporters of the king at St Neots they would have kept their opinions to themselves during the early war years as there were Roundhead soldiers in the town for several months. In 1643 some of the troops commanded by Sir Edward Montague were 'guarding St Needs' and evidently fearing attacks from the king's forces from across the river, because part of the bridge had been converted into a drawbridge to prevent access from the west.

Although many people in Huntingdonshire supported Oliver Cromwell because he was the local Member of Parliament and a dominant figure in the Parliamentary Army, there were many others who did not. When the king travelled from Huntingdon 'unto St Eaotes' on his way to Woburn in 1645 he gathered several hundred recruits to his cause en route, making his force so strong that a troop of Roundheads who were following after him were discouraged and retreated.

St Neots was spared a battle on that occasion but three years later, in 1648, it was the scene of a skirmish which merited the publication of a special pamphlet to describe it. A party of about one hundred Royalist cavalry under Henry Rich, Earl of Holland, having suffered defeat in a battle at Kingston-on-Thames, retreated northwards. On their way they were joined by several more officers and soldiers, including the Duke of Buckingham, the Earl of Peterborough and a Dutchman, Colonel Dolbier.

They arrived in St Neots late one night, by then some 300 strong, and the Earl of Holland assured the townspeople that they intended no harm but simply required somewhere to rest for the night. The soldiers made their camp on the Market Square leaving a small party to guard the bridge, and the officers retired to various inns to sleep. The largest local inn at the time was *The Cross Keys* and it is likely that the Earl of Holland would have taken a room there. The Duke of Buckingham did not stay in the town but went to 'a gentleman's house' a few miles away, perhaps Paxton Hall at Little Paxton.

Early the following morning a troop of about one hundred Roundhead soldiers arrived, led by Colonel Scroop, having pursued the Royalists from Kingston. They easily overcame the party of men guarding the bridge and advanced into St Neots to attack the troops on the square. The Royalists, although they outnumbered their assailants, were caught unprepared and had no time to engage in the lengthy process of loading their muskets, so they had to fight with swords. Being still drowsy from sleep they were no match for the Parliamentarians and the battle was short and sharp. There were few fatal casualties, only four officers and eight Royalists being killed, with the Roundheads losing only four men. The Royalists, including most of the other officers, were then taken prisoner. The Earl of Holland, roused from his bed at the inn, was reputedly so unprepared that he did not have time to dress properly and he was taken prisoner in his undergarments! The Duke of Buckingham, who had arrived late on the scene from his out-of-town location, escaped with about one hundred soldiers and was able to make his way to France, but the Earl of Peterborough, who also fled from the battle, was captured later.

A Great

VICTORY

Obtained by

COLLONELL SCROOPE

Againſt the

Duke of BUCKINGHAM, at Saint
Needs in Huntingtonſhire. On Munday
July the 10th. 1648.

Where was ſlain	The Duke of Buckhingham fled with 200 Horſe.
Col. Dolbier, Quartermaſter Generall. 3 Officers more. 8 Troopers.	Taken beſides. 200 Horſe, 150 Fire Armes, 100 Great Saddles, Powder ſome pounds.
Taken Priſoners: Earl of Holland, 300 Officers and Gentlemen, 120 Troopers.	Silver, and gold and ſtore of other good plunder. The Earle of Hollands blew Ribbon and his George.

LONDON,
Printed for the generall ſatisfaction of moderate men.
M DC XL VIII.

59   The cover of a pamphlet describing the Battle of St Neots, 1648.

The jubilant Roundheads marched their prisoners down St Neots High Street and locked them in the parish church. They were later taken to Hitchin but what became of them after that is not known. The Earl of Holland was sent to Warwick Castle to be held and the following year he was tried and executed.

The pamphlet which was published to celebrate the battle of St Neots listed a number of items which were taken by the victors and these included 200 horses, 150 firearms, 'silver and gold and store of other good plunder', and the Earl of Holland's Order of St George medallion on its 'blew ribbon'. As well as the military personnel who were captured there were a number of civilian servants, including the Earl's personal surgeon.

After the execution of Charles I in 1649 England became a Commonwealth under the command of Oliver Cromwell as Lord Protector. He was obviously not satisfied that all opposition had been completely quashed and a strong army was maintained. A letter from an officer in Colonel John Okey's regiment, written in 1650, stated that for 23 weeks the men were at St Neots and Kimbolton and later in the year they spent another eight weeks in the area. At Huntingdon there was the Committee for Sequestrations from where men went out to confiscate property belonging to Royalist sympathisers, either then leasing it back to them for a high rent or leasing it to those who had supported the Parliamentary cause.

Oliver Cromwell was a grave-natured and deeply religious man, devoted to the Puritan ethic. He abhorred the elaborate rituals of the Established Church and the colourful trimmings which accompanied them. Accordingly, his followers set about completing the desecration of churches which Henry VIII's reformers had begun in the previous century. Those churches whose stained glass windows had managed to survive earlier destruction found their windows shattered by Cromwell's men, who also smashed or defaced carvings and removed vestments and holy vessels. The Puritans vetoed the ringing of bells and the use of stone altars which they said were redolent of sacrifice. All over the country stone altars were replaced by wooden Communion tables, and in Huntingdonshire the only stone *mensa* to survive is the one at Oldhurst. At St Neots the 17th-century Communion table, originally in the chancel, is now in a side aisle. It is carved with masks and acanthus leaves and is a particularly fine example.

In many parishes the vicars were replaced by 'Registers' and this happened locally. According to church records 'John Luke of Eynesbury, gent, was sworn Register of the severall parishes of St Neotts and Eynesbury' in October 1653. The church registers were kept faithfully by him until 1657, but they ceased to be written up from then until 1660 as far as Eynesbury was concerned. No records at all for the years of the war or the Commonwealth appear to have been kept at St Neots.

At Eaton Socon the minister was Robert White until 1645 and he was reputedly a staunch Royalist. Thomas Becke was provisionally presented to the living in 1647 but he too was suspected of Royalist leanings and of being too fond of the rituals of the Established Church. Despite criticism from his superiors he was officially installed in 1659 and is said to have been very popular with his parishioners which suggest that the people of Eaton Socon were also traditionalists at heart. The Eaton church records were carefully kept during the war years but from 1650 onwards they were badly neglected. In 1650 and 1652 no baptisms at all were recorded and only two were entered in 1651. From 1653 onwards small numbers were recorded under the heading 'Borne' instead of 'Baptized' and the older heading only returned in 1660.

Among other rituals condemned by the Puritans were the ceremonies associated with Christmas and May Day. Maypoles were deemed to be akin to heathen idols and Cromwell ordered their removal. Since Eaton Socon has a long tradition of maypole dancing it is probable that there was a pole there which had to be taken down, and there would have been no more Morris dancing and May Games throughout the neighbourhood. Cromwell also disapproved of convivial drinking and, although he could not ban drinking altogether since beer was the staple beverage of the time, he laid heavy taxes on alehouse landlords and innkeepers. As singing and music in such places was also banned, it must have been a very dull time for local residents.

In 1657 a group of Cromwell's supporters proposed that he should become king, a proposal which was vehemently opposed by people of all ranks, including 'many godly and well-affected people in the county of Bedford ...Olney in the county of Buckingham ... and St Neots in the county of Huntingdon'. To give him his due, this proposal was also condemned by Cromwell himself, but the fact that it was put forward indicates the country's nostalgia for the Monarchy. After Oliver Cromwell's death and an unsuccessful attempt by his son to follow in his footsteps, Prince Charles, the exiled son of the beheaded king, was invited to return to England and become Charles II.

The Restoration of the Monarchy in 1660 meant a gradual return to normality, with the maypoles going up again and the song and dance resuming. Several innkeepers celebrated by renaming their houses and one of these was in South Street, St Neots, where an inn formerly called *The Wyldeman* became *The Kings Head*. Until recently its inn sign carried a picture of Charles II and it seems a pity that the sign now bears a picture of another monarch.

60 The Kings Head Inn *with its original sign.*

61   The Kings Head Inn, *South Street, St Neots.*

During the years that followed many houses, shops and licensed premises in the St Neots area were rebuilt. When the Royal Commissioners for Historical Monuments surveyed St Neots and Eynesbury in 1926 they identified a number of late 17th-century buildings, although they missed several others where facades of 19th-century brick concealed timber-framed structures. They noted, for example, an old timber-framed house in Huntingdon Street, on the corner of East Street, which has since been demolished, but failed to see that the house next to it, Cressener House, was of a similar date under its brickwork. Hall Place in Cambridge Street was also faced in brick over timbering as were buildings in St Mary's Street, Eynesbury. The former Rectory at Eynesbury is also partially 17th-

century, but may have older structures within it. According to legend there were soldiers billeted there either during or after the Civil War, which—if true—would suggest an earlier date. Legend also says that the building is haunted and some of the residents who have lived there since it became a private house have reported hearing strange noises. One person described them as sounding like horses hooves on cobbles, and voices talking and laughing. Two former occupiers also claim to have seen a figure in 17th-century dress in one of the bedrooms!

Along the Great North Road in Eaton Socon there are more 17th-century buildings, including *The Waggon and Horses* public house, and Ford House at Eaton Ford probably dates from the same period.

62   Hall Place, Cambridge Street, a 17th-century building faced in 19th-century brick with later extension on the left.

63   A 17th-century building which once stood in Huntingdon Street, St Neots, on the corner of East Street.

64 *Cressener House in Huntingdon Street, undergoing restoration.*

65 *During the restoration of Cressener House timbers in the front wall were revealed.*

66 *17th-century cottages which once stood in Brook Street.*

67 *A house in Montagu Street, Eynesbury, probably 17th-century, before restoration.*

68 *Eynesbury Old Rectory, said to be haunted by Civil War soldiers.*

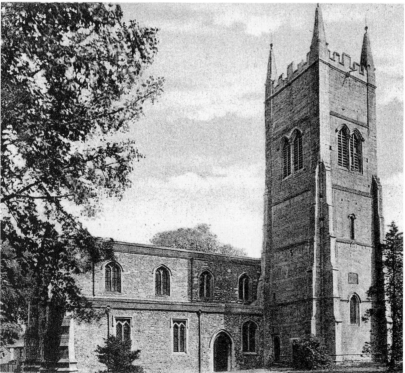

69 *Eynesbury church from the south, with its tower rebuilt in 1687.*

70 *Eaton Ford House, Eaton Ford, from a drawing made in the early 19th century. Since then its rendering has been removed to reveal its timber-framed construction.*

71 *Eaton Socon village in the early 20th century, with 17th-century buildings including the* Waggon and Horses *public house on the left.*

Number of Hearths	Number of houses in each category		
	St Neots, 1674	Eynesbury, 1674	Eaton Socon, 1671
1	131	58	148
2	38	29	21
3	16	10	13
4	21	3	4
5	13	2	7
6	5	2	4
7	3	2	-
8	4	-	-
9	-	-	2
10	1	-	1
11	-	-	-
12	1	-	-
13	-	-	-
14	1	-	2
15	1	-	-
TOTAL	**235**	**106**	**202**

72 A chart showing the distribution of hearths recorded in the Hearth Tax Returns in the 1670s.

Among the after-effects of the Civil War and the Commonwealth period was a need to raise money by taxation, to replenish depleted Royal finances. A Hearth Tax was imposed in several years, on the principle that those people with the most fireplaces in their homes could afford to pay the most. A study of Hearth Tax Returns in general shows that the majority of houses had only one hearth and from four to five hearths indicated an affluent middle-class household. The returns for St Neots show that in 1674 there were 235 houses in the town, over half of them with one hearth apiece. Half of these were lived in by people paying no tax because of poverty. At the other end of the scale there were four houses with ten or more hearths. Mr. Woodstock lived in a house with no fewer than 15 hearths! Eynesbury had no very large houses, according to the Hearth Tax Returns, the largest being one with seven hearths, occupied by Mrs. Norman. The pattern of poverty at Eynesbury was similar to that at St Neots, with half the total of 106 houses having only one hearth and half of the occupants of them being too poor to pay.

The figures for Eaton Socon are interesting but slightly misleading as they include a number of hamlets within the parish, only Wyboston and Begwary being recorded separately. This gave a total of 202 houses with almost three-quarters of them having only one hearth. Many of the one-hearth homes were probably in the hamlets and most of their occupants were able to pay tax. Two houses at Eaton had 14 hearths each, one occupied by Gaius Squire, lord of the manor, and the other one the residence of William Gery, lord of the manor of Bushmead.

By this time St Neots was able to provide adequately for its poor, although during the early years of the century the parish had relied to some extent on bequests from local benefactors to supplement its resources. In

1620, for instance, Joan Cromwell left 40s. a year for the 'poor, impotent and lame people of St Neots' and in 1648 Hugh Wye left £40 which was to be spent in purchasing land, the rent from it providing twopenny loaves for the poor. By 1678, however, an effective system of rate levying was in operation, with charges on houses from 2d. to 2s. 4d., and on land according to acreage. A farmer at Wintringham paid 2s. 6d. for his farm and Samuel Paine, who also owned land at Wintringham, paid 15s. 2d. Payments to the poor recorded in 1673 show that, of the 40 listed recipients of relief, 21 were widows. There were also a number of children, mostly orphans, described as various people's 'cheldren', 'childe' or 'sunn' and there was one entry regarding a woman's 'basterd childe'. One widow was allowed money for looking after a child who was not her own but 'one lookin to hur'. Only six of the 40 paupers were men and they were probably elderly or

73 *Local tokens issued in lieu of coinage. The top row shows tokens issued by the Overseers of the Poor, which depict women making lace. (From G.C. Gorham's* History of St Neots, *1824.)*

infirm. Although the average sum paid out was only 1s. 6d. a week, contemporary price lists show that it would have been sufficient to buy two pounds of meat, a pound of cheese, a large loaf, small quantities of sugar, soap and butter and still leave enough over for a pint of ale and an ounce of tobacco!

Although it seems from the Hearth Tax Returns that there were no very wealthy people in Eynesbury, the parish was able to embark on the rebuilding of the church tower in the 1680s. A document held at Lincoln recorded in 1684

> that the steeple of the church, having been a broach or spire steeple, and very decrepit and ruinous, did very lately fall down ... the same steeple having been built in most unusual manner betwixt the south aisle and the body of the said church, and in the fall thereof did beat down not only a great part of the middle aisle but also the south aisle, whereby the said church is become useless ...

The parishioners were asking leave at that point to cover the structure with boards until proper repairs could be carried out, which they announced their intention of doing as soon as possible.

By the 1680s spires were no longer in fashion and the replacement was constructed as a tower. It bears a plaque inscribed '1687 HENREY ASHLEY THOMAS RUTLAND CHUCHWARDNES' obviously carved by someone whose spelling was not very good. Mr. Ashley and Mr. Rutland would have been responsible for organising the rebuilding and also collecting the funds to pay for it. Many sets of initials are inscribed directly into the stonework of the tower and these may indicate names of those who subscribed towards the rebuilding, because one set of initials, 'T.K.' is accompanied by the date 1687.

Another local church which bears 17th-century inscriptions is the one at St Neots. Incised or moulded into the lead of the nave roof are three names and the date 1674. One of the names is Scroop, which was also the name of the victorious leader at the Battle of St Neots during the Civil War. There is a local legend to the effect that his soldiers, having conducted their Royalist prisoners to the church, discharged their muskets into the air in celebration of their victory. Perhaps the churchwardens of St Neots persuaded Colonel Scroop to contribute to the roof repairs as an apology, and he agreed to do so provided his name was recorded in lead!

Chapter 6

Stagecoaches and Enclosure—1700 to 1800

The 18th century was an age of new ideas and the changes that took place as a result. One of the first ideas to take root locally was the notion that it would be better to house all the recipients of poor relief in one building rather than leaving them to cope in their own homes. In 1707 John Dryden left £100 in his will to buy land for the benefit of the poor and this may have led to the establishment of the first poorhouse or workhouse at St Neots, since it is known to have been in existence by 1722. According to an old almanac it was situated at the northern end of New Street, near the entrance to the Common, although by 1730 the churchwardens were renting property in Church Street from Mr. Pulleyn of Old Hall Place, for use as a workhouse.

As in the previous century the women and girls housed in the building made pillow lace to raise money towards their own support and receipts dated 1711 show that thread, pins and bobbins were bought from a local dealer and lengths of lace were sold back to him. Lacemaking also continued at Eaton Socon, where a workhouse was established by 1719. The inmates at Eaton Socon were compelled to wear badges marked with the letter 'P' to denote that they were paupers.

St Neots seems to have treated its poor with a little more understanding as they were not required to wear badges and the food provided in the workhouse was probably superior to that eaten by many residents outside it. Purchases recorded in the accounts for the Church Street workhouse included large quantities of meat, cheese and fruit, and clothing was provided on an individual basis. 'Goody Watts' had a shift bought for her on one occasion, 'Widow Sanders' had an apron and a Miss or Mrs. Goodjohn got 'a pare of stays'. When Susan Fox was married a local seamstress was paid to make her 'a gown and peaticoat'.

Although the workhouse was in use, the almshouses in Brook Street continued to be occupied. According to C.F. Tebbutt there was a reference to almshouses as early as 1485 and they were in Brook Street by 1693, next to the tall building which was later the *Bushel and Strike* public house. As there was a further reference to them in 1775 they must have continued to house the poor until then.

By 1700 a few turnpikes had been set across the main roads, but the tolls raised by them were evidently insufficient to maintain good travelling conditions. Daniel Defoe, writing in 1724, described the stretch of main road between Biggleswade and Buckden as 'a most frightful way' and said that travellers often turned off it into private land to avoid the 'sloughs and holes which no horse could wade through'. Eventually an Act was passed authorising the setting up of Turnpike Trusts to manage the collection of tolls and the distribution of part of the money on road maintenance. In 1725 a Trust was established to manage the Great North Road between Biggleswade and Alconbury, and several more bars were placed across the road, these being later replaced by tollgates with cottages beside them to house the tollgate keepers. It was proposed at one time that a gate should be erected at Eaton Socon but the toll point was eventually placed further north, on the parish boundary between Little Paxton and Southoe.

The keeper of the Southoe gate throughout most of the 18th century was Francis Loxley. He was a keen gardener and also a follower of the Cambridgeshire Hunt and he combined his two passions by clipping a bush which stood beside the road into a topiary version of a horse and rider. During the hunting season the rider was dressed in a red coat and it became a well-known landmark for travellers.

Another Turnpike Trust was founded in 1772 to manage part of the road between Cambridge and St Neots, and one of the toll-gate cottages associated with the road still stands near Weald House to the east of the town.

A tollgate once existed at the New Street entrance to St Neots Common, but this was a private venture and the tolls demanded went into the funds of the holders of Common Rights. Private landowners were also quick to take advantage of the Act to make money for themselves and according to one source a private tollgate was once set up near the mill at Little Paxton by the mill owner, Anderson Pelham.

Improved roads meant more travelling and the number of coaches and carriages passing through St Neots and Eaton Socon increased. There had been coaches on the roads in the late 17th century but it was during the 18th century that coaching reached its 'Golden Age' when the stagecoach was introduced. It was found that a constant fast speed could only be achieved by changing the teams of horses which pulled coaches at intervals of about ten or twelve miles. In 1734 the contractor system was evolved by which innkeepers at suitable intervals along the route undertook to provide fresh horses for the coaches. The advantage to the innkeepers, apart from the fees received for providing this service, was an increase in trade as passengers bought drinks or food while the horses were being changed and sometimes stayed overnight in order to break a long journey. Overnight stays were probably frequent because in 1754 the journey from London to Edinburgh took at least eight days.

The first regular long-distance coach journeys went from London to York in 1706 and by 1754 coaches were travelling as far as Edinburgh. At the height of stagecoach activity there were coaches passing through Eaton Socon about 20 times a day, some of them going straight up the Great North Road after changing horses at *The White Horse* and others taking the loop through St Neots. At *The Cross Keys Inn* mail was collected as well as passengers and the evidence suggests that horses may have been changed there instead of at Eaton Socon on these particular routes.

This new form of transport brought more trade to the town as well as benefiting the innkeepers because there was work for horse-breeders, farriers and harness-makers too. St Neots and Eaton Socon both prospered because of stagecoaches and must have been envied by the traders of Eynesbury, which had no long-distance routes passing through it.

Travelling had its hazards in the 18th century, just as in earlier times. Stagecoaches sometimes overturned through being driven too fast, or lost a wheel because of poor maintenance. There was also the danger of highway robbery, for ordinary horse riders as well as coach passengers. One particularly gruesome crime is said to have taken place in the early 18th century on the road between Cambridge and St Neots.

A young woman, having collected a large sum of money, was riding back to St Neots. Fearing that she might be robbed she had concealed the money bag in her hair, piling up her long tresses over it and pinning them tightly before putting on her kerchief. On her way she met another rider who offered to escort her home. As he was a neighbour whom she knew well, a local butcher and innkeeper, she accepted gratefully, but made the mistake of telling him about her money and how she had hidden it. This resulted in her death, and the murderer, anxious to escape from the scene, did not stop to remove the money but chopped off her head and stowed it in his saddlebag.

A short time afterwards two other horsemen came along, a gentleman and his servant,

74   *The public wharf in Brook Street, St Neots in about 1910. The steps down to Henbrook are in the foreground. On the left are* The Bushel and Strike *and* The White Swan.

75   The White Horse, *Eaton Socon, in the 1930s.*

The Hotel, Eaton Socon.

and found the decapitated corpse. The gentleman, obviously quick-thinking, sent his servant on ahead telling him to contact the first person he overtook, who was likely to be the murderer, and accompany him wherever he was going. This was done and the servant and the butcher rode into St Neots together. Once there the servant called the local constable and the saddlebag was searched, revealing its grisly contents. What makes the story really horrific is that the head was recognised by the constable as being that of his own wife! If this story is true, the villain of the piece may have kept the butcher's shop shown in illustration No. 54, which was next to an inn.

Another of the ideas which took root in the 18th century was the concept of education for all classes of society, not just the sons of the gentry, and the first Charity Schools were founded. In 1736 a school for '35 poor boys' was established at St Neots and although at that stage it was evidently not considered necessary to educate girls, by the end of the century there was a school for 'poor children' which may indicate that some girls were included. Classes were held at first in the Jesus Chapel of St Neots Church but after 1745 they moved elsewhere. In 1760 Alderman Newton of Leicester left money in his will for the benefit of schools in Huntingdonshire and the school at St Neots

76 The Cross Keys, *Market Square, St Neots, in the 1930s.*

received £26 to clothe as well as educate poor boys. There are no references to a Charity School at Eynesbury at this period but there may have been one at Eaton Socon because James Livett was referred to as a schoolmaster there in the late 18th century.

Agriculture was the principal occupation of most local people but the idea of industrialisation was growing and that had its impact too. In the early years of the century corn-milling was the only industrial process being carried out in St Neots but in 1735 Joseph Eayre came to the town and built a bell foundry in the lane which had once led to the priory. The building is shown on the map dated 1757 which has

already been mentioned and it can also be seen on Jeffreys' county map of 1768, in the background of the picture of St Neots bridge which decorates the base of the map. Bells were cast in Mr. Eayre's foundry for many years, some of which still hang in the churches of Huntingdonshire and neighbouring counties. Joseph Eayre himself died in 1772 but the business was carried on by Edward Arnold and later by Robert Taylor.

Another local industry which grew up during the 18th century was that of brewing and malting. A large maltings once existed in Cambridge Street, St Neots, on the site later occupied by a private school and later still by a

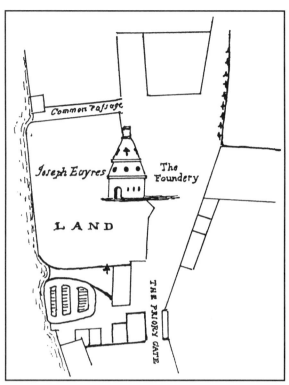

77 *Part of a map dated 1757, showing Joseph Eayres' bell foundry.*

78 *St Neots bridge in 1768, from Jeffreys' county map, with the bell foundry visible through the left-hand arch.*

79   The Priory Brewery in 1920. Only the barley kiln and part of the building attached to it remain.

car park. At Eaton Socon 'Maltmans Gardens' was marked on the 1768 map, and a malting was referred to at Eynesbury in the early 18th century. The product of these businesses, however, was supplied initially to the individual inns and alehouses for them to brew beers and ales on their own premises, and it was not until the latter end of the 18th century that the idea of wholesale brewing caught on. It may have been Samuel Emery who began the first brewery in St Neots. He purchased the *Bull Inn* on the Market Square together with an adjacent public house and combined their two brewhouses in order to brew in large quantities. When Samuel died in 1788 he left the inn to his daughters but the brewery to his son, who was then listed as a brewer in the directory dated 1792. Samuel Emery junior sold the property to William Foster and by the end of the century Foster was supplying ale and beer to three local licensed premises, all owned by him.

The other brewery which was established at about the same time was a purpose-built one, constructed on the site of the old priory and called, not surprisingly, the Priory Brewery. Its builder was a man with a name confusingly similar to his rival—William Fowler—and it was erected between 1780 and 1782. It covered a wide area and as well as the brewhouse there was a malting, a kiln for drying barley, stabling and storehouses. Mr. Fowler lived in a house on the site, which had already been there when he acquired the property. The barley kiln survives, known locally as 'The Oast House', and Mr. Fowler's house, but the other buildings were demolished in the 1960s.

Brewers and maltsters would have had plenty of outlets for their products, as during the 18th century 32 licensed premises were recorded at St Neots, 11 at Eaton Socon and two at least at Eynesbury. There were probably many more for which records have not survived.

80 A 19th-century drawing of The Cock Inn *at Eaton Socon.*

81 Plan of The Cock Inn *from a sale catalogue, 1845.*

A Valuation dated 1809 lists several that were probably in existence well before that date. Of those appearing by name in 18th-century documents 28 have since disappeared, although they were replaced by others, and many more opened during the century which followed. The most notable casualties were *The Cock Inn* at Eaton Socon and *The George* in St Neots High Street.

The Cock Inn stood to the north of Eaton Socon church, on the corner of Peppercorns Lane, and was a highly respected hostelry in the 18th century with a reputation for good food and comfortable accommodation. Viscount Torrington, who visited the inn several times in the 1790s, wrote complimentary remarks about it in his diaries and described Eaton itself as 'a gay village with a very fine large church'. He passed through St Neots on one occasion but did not sample the inns there. At the time there was a great fair taking place which included an elephant and a tableau depicting the guillotining of the King of France. The Viscount disapproved strongly of the latter,

EATON SOCON, BEDFORDSHIRE.

MOST EXTENSIVE

FREEHOLD BUSINESS PREMISES,

NOW USED, AND SO WELL KNOWN AS

"THE COCK INN", AT EATON,

Fifty-five Miles from London, on the Great North Road.

WILL BE SOLD BY AUCTION, BY

WILLIAM MEDLAND,

On THURSDAY, the 11th day of SEPTEMBER, 1845,

On the Premises, at Six o'Clock in the Evening,

In Two Lots, by direction of the Assignees of the Estate & Effects of Henry Decimus Walker.

Lot 1—Is the HOUSE, which is in a very pleasant [Situation,] and has been so long justly appreciated by the Nobility and Gentry for its retirement and first-rate accommodation.

The principal part of the **South Wing** comprises on the **Ground Floor**, a Portico Entrance, Hall and Passages, which are laid down with Yorkshire Slabs, and lighted by a Stained Glass Fan. There are Five Dining and Drawing Rooms of good dimensions and well proportioned, averaging about 16 feet square; little Parlour, and excellent and well arranged Bar, large Kitchen, Waiters' and other Pantries, cool Larder, Two Stair Cases, and well fitted up underground Wine and Beer Cellars, of proper temperature;

On the First Floor is an excellent Landing, Seven first-rate Bed Rooms, Three Dressing Rooms and Water Closet.

On the Second Floor is the Green Room, 18 feet by 19 feet, and Ten other Bed Rooms.

The North Wing comprises good Dining Room, Two large Bed Rooms, Dressing ditto, and Two Attics, Ostler's Room, Scullery, with Pump and Sink therein, and Chamber over;

THE OUTHOUSES,

cool Dairy, Laundry, 28 feet 9 inches by 14 feet 6 inches, Coal, Knife, and Boot Places, Wood Barn, and every other Convenience.

An enclosed and private YARD, with Entrances to different parts of the House, with Veranda Top.

THE OTHER OUT-DOOR ARRANGEMENTS

ARE EQUALLY ADVANTAGEOUS, AND EMBRACE

STABLING FOR SIXTY HORSES,

besides Six loose Boxes, well fitted up and ventilated; Lock-up Houses for Eight Carriages, Granaries, Harness Rooms, and Ostlery.

The Yards are Paved, in which are force and other Pumps, with excellent Wells of Water, in convenient Situations.

Drying Grounds and Garden on the North Side,

WHICH ADJOIN A PRIVATE ROADWAY.

The House has Seven Bay Windows in Front, is approached by a circular Carriage Drive, with a pleasing and attractive SHRUBBERY intersecting it and the Great North Road, and there are two small GARDENS also in Front.

82 Sale details of The Cock Inn, *1845.*

83   The building on the corner of High Street and Huntingdon Street, formerly The George Inn, *photographed in 1899.*

writing 'Is not this a *bad* exhibition for the lower people?' Perhaps he thought it would give them ideas! *The Cock Inn* was also used as a meeting place for several local bodies, including the Turnpike Trustees for the Biggleswade road, and it is thought that meetings of the Eaton Socon manor court were also held there. Unlike *The White Horse* it was never a coaching inn, catering instead for a higher class clientèle with private carriages. It also hired out horses and post-chaises.

The George at St Neots was built in about 1740 by Joseph Eayre of the bell foundry and was designed as an inn with assembly rooms at first-floor level. The inn did not function for very long, being delicensed and converted into small tenements in 1773, but the assembly rooms were well used for meetings and, in later years, dances and balls also took place there. The

building still stands on the corner of Huntingdon Street but its ground floor has been altered several times to accommodate shops. The main assembly room originally had a very fine plaster ceiling which included an unusual suspended dome but a few years ago the dome was found to be cracked and had to be removed for safety reasons. One of the traditional stories about *The George* says that John Wesley, one of the founders of Methodism, preached at meetings in its assembly rooms.

Wesley certainly visited St Neots several times and was indirectly responsible for the formation of the first Methodist group in the town in 1775. Local people who had heard John Wesley preach at a meeting at Godmanchester resolved to form a similar group at St Neots and in 1775 the St Neots Methodists came into being and welcomed Wesley to a

84 *The Old Meeting House, St Neots, from a 19th-century drawing.*

85 *A view of St Neots looking north from the church tower in about 1870. The High Street runs left to right and the Old Meeting House can be seen on the left of the photograph, in the middle distance.*

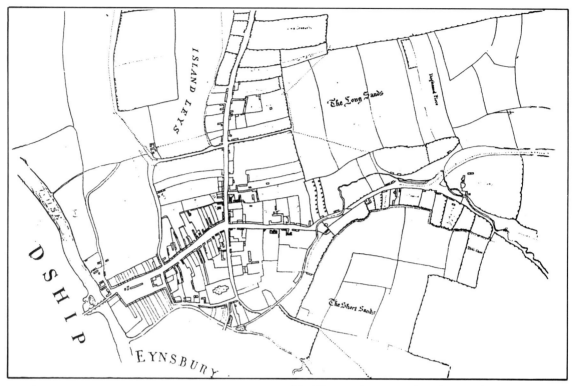

86   *The town of St Neots in the 18th century, based on the Inclosure Map of 1771.*

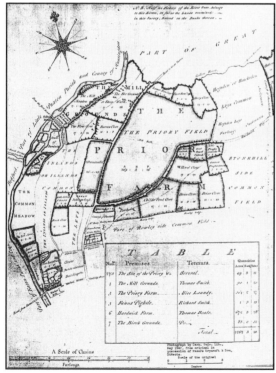

87   *A map dated 1757 showing Priory Farm, acquired by Owsley Rowley in 1793.*

meeting in the same year. Over the ensuing 15 years Wesley made eight further visits to the town, sometimes preaching in a barn in East Street and sometimes in the maltings in Cambridge Street. One meeting took place at five o'clock in the morning 'to enable the labouring classes to attend before going to work'. There were also Methodists meeting at Eaton Socon by 1782.

Other nonconformist groups were formed even earlier in neighbouring villages, and these included the Congregationalists or Independents. There was a 'Meeting' at Hail Weston by the end of the 17th century and some time after 1701 the Meeting moved to St Neots. The Old Meeting House is believed to have been built between 1710 and 1720 and it stood to the north of High Street, set back from it, on a site which is now behind the United Reformed Church. It was a fine classically-styled building with a pedimented roof-line and pilasters on the front. It survived until the late 1960s when it was unfortunately destroyed by fire. There was no local Baptist church during this period but a number of local people attended Baptist meetings in neighbouring villages such as Hail Weston and Little Staughton.

It was in the 1770s that another new idea which was sweeping the country began to have its effect locally. A study of farming methods had been taking place for several years and there was a growing feeling that the old method of strip-farming was time-consuming and inefficient. By the mid-18th century some landowners had already begun exchanging strips in order to create blocks of land which could be farmed more easily, and it was generally felt that the time had come to abandon strip-farming altogether and re-arrange the land into more compact areas which could be cultivated by each farmer independently. As this new system involved the abolition of land laws which had operated for many centuries, the changes could only be achieved by Act of Parliament, with each parish formulating its own Act.

The Inclosure Act for St Neots was presented in 1770 and the following year, after a survey, the Inclosure Award was drawn up, defining the areas to be allocated to each land-owner in lieu of strips. Perhaps because this was one of the early enclosures, it was only the arable land which was re-arranged and the commons and Lammas Meadow remained under the old system. Those who held Common Rights still retained the privilege of grazing their livestock on the commons and cutting a strip of grass for hay from the meadow. In the Inclosure Award a total of 154 Common Rights was confirmed and the number remains the same to the present day. The map, which was drawn up to show the various allotments of land, also shows the buildings which were in St Neots in 1771 and, although some are missing where the map is torn, there appear to be between 150 and 160 properties, which means that every one of the buildings had a Common Right attached to it. Houses which were built later did not have such rights.

Eynesbury was enclosed in 1795 and Eaton Socon in 1797. In both parishes the commons and meadows were included in the re-arrangement of land and the Commoners lost their rights of grazing.

Rather better preserved than the Inclosure Map are several maps dated 1757 showing the estate of Sir Stephen Anderson, who had acquired the demesne lands of the priory once held by Francis Williams. The maps show the former priory site and properties on the north side of the Market Square, farms at Wintringham and Monks Hardwick, and the Priory Farm at the northern end of Huntingdon Street. Priory Farm was purchased in 1793 by Owsley Rowley, who built a farmhouse there and later a gentleman's residence. The farmland surrounding the house became parkland and was suitably landscaped with trees. At the top of Priory Hill an ice-house was built below ground in which ice, collected from the ponds in winter, was stored for use in the summer months. This small domed and brick-built structure, with its tunnel-like entrance, gave rise to a local myth that it was the opening to a tunnel which once linked the hill to St Neots Priory!

Another interesting 18th-century map shows that there were then several buildings on the Market Square at St Neots. The cartouche at the base of the map shows what they looked like. Some had open fronts and were arranged in a row facing north, and these were the shops known as 'Butchers' Shambles'. The same writer who described the old priory gatehouse also wrote about these buildings, which included a Butter House, a house for 'Stall Geer' and several other small tradesmen's shops. All these buildings were demolished in the early 19th century.

Several 18th-century buildings do still remain locally, as well as buildings which were altered or added to during the period. *The White Horse* at Eaton Socon and *The Cross Keys* at St Neots were both re-fronted in the 18th century and several smaller local buildings had brick facings added to them. The finest 18th-century building to be seen locally is Brook House in

88   *A mid-18th-century map of St Neots Market Square, with north at the bottom, showing the buildings on the square.*

Brook Street, St Neots. It is a beautifully-proportioned, symmetrical house with red brick walls and a hipped roof. It was probably built for a member of the Reynolds family of Paxton Hall, since it was the property of Mrs. Reynolds in 1743.

In 1798 an event took place in Eynesbury which was to bring the village country-wide notoriety. In a small cottage in the lane leading to Eynesbury Rectory, James Toller was born.

He grew to be 8ft.6in. tall by the time he was in his teens and was known as the Eynesbury Giant. After a short spell in the army he travelled the country being exhibited at fairs and markets, and was presented to royalty on one occasion. His health, however, was not good and he returned to Eynesbury where he died at the age of twenty. His body was buried inside Eynesbury church instead of in the churchyard, for fear that grave-robbers would try to exhume his body.

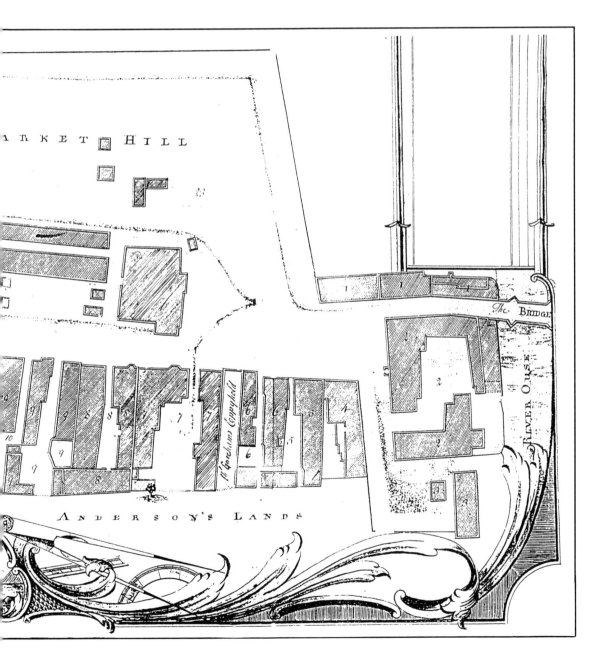

89   Above. *Brook House, Brook Street, St Neots.*

90   Below left. *Rectory Lane, Eynesbury. In one of the cottages at the left, now demolished, James Toller was born in 1798.*

91   Below right. *A 19th-century impression of James Toller, the Eynesbury Giant.*

Chapter 7

Growth and Change—1800 to 1900

The growth of industrialisation which began in the 18th century continued in the 19th. In 1808 two brothers named Henry and Sealy Fourdrinier bought the corn mill which stood near the boundary between St Neots and Little Paxton and converted it from a flour-producing mill to one producing paper. Until the early 19th century paper had been made in single sheets but the Fourdrinier brothers invented a process by which paper could be made in a continuous roll and it was at the St Neots mill that this process was first used. At first the machines which manufactured the paper were powered by water but as production increased the water power was supplemented by steam turbines.

The Fourdriniers were brilliant inventors but unfortunately they were less successful as businessmen. They did not take out sufficiently

92   *An imaginary bird's-eye view of the Paper Mills in 1888.*

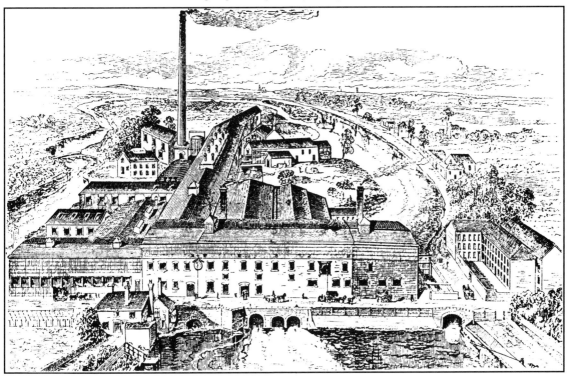

93 *Duloe windmill, Eaton Socon, in the 1930s.*

known as Duloe Mill because it was on the Duloe road. It burned down in 1815 and was replaced by the one which still stands on the site, but now, minus its sails, has been converted into a private house. Other windmills were situated in Cambridge Street, St Neots and next to the paper mills. Towards the latter end of the 19th century a steam-powered mill operated behind property in the south-west corner of the Market Square and was known as the John Bull Mill.

The breweries established in the 18th century expanded steadily and were joined by other, smaller concerns. William Foster's brewery on the Market Square was purchased by James Paine in 1831 and gradually acquired more tied houses in which to sell its ales and beers. The building which still fronts onto the square bears the date 1831, which is when James Paine became its owner, but old engravings of the square dated between 1820 and 1824 show that this imposing building was already there by then and must have been built by William Foster.

The Priory Brewery was also sold in the early years of the century, passing from the Fowler family to John Day of Bedford in 1814. At the time of the sale the Fowlers owned a total of 24 licensed premises, although only five of them were in St Neots, two at Eaton Socon and one at Eaton Ford. John Day gradually added to the number and between 1818 and 1839 the total increased to 63, with 15 of them in St Neots.

One of Mr. Day's first actions was to demolish the gatehouse which was the last remaining relic of St Neots Priory. The lane in which it was situated was called Bell Lane at that time, because of the bell foundry, and the writer whose description of the gatehouse was quoted earlier apparently approved of its demolition, since he wrote that 'the Bell Lane being widened by J.H. Day, Esq., was another great improvement'. There were no reservations in those days about destroying ancient monuments and Mr. Day's priority was to provide a better road for his brewery drays.

comprehensive patents to protect their invention which was copied and amended by other manufacturers with devastating results. The brothers found themselves being overtaken by competitors and ended up bankrupt, the paper-making business being taken over by Matthew Towgood. Mr. Towgood operated the mill for several years, as did his sons after him, but in the early 1880s the business closed down. It had provided work for many local men and women, and to safeguard their jobs it was taken over in 1888 by a consortium of local men under the title of the St Neots Paper Mill Company. They took no profit from it for themselves for some considerable time in order to get the business on its feet again.

Corn milling still went on locally as well, with a water wheel providing power for a mill at Eaton Socon, erected in 1847 on the site of an older version, and several windmills. One windmill stood at the top of Mill Hill at Eaton,

94 Staff of Paine's flour mill in Bedford Street, St Neots, in about 1900.

95 Paine & Co's premises on St Neots Market Square, behind which was the brewery.

96 Left. *An imaginary bird's-eye view of Paine & Co's brewery and associated buildings, drawn in the mid-19th century.*

97 Below. *An engraving of St Neots Market Square from a drawing by John Surman Austin in 1853. Paine & Co's brewery is in the middle distance, right of centre.*

98 Right. *The Market Square in the early 1800s, showing Paine's building on the right.*

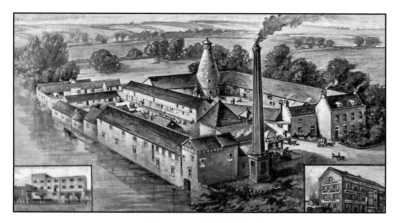

99 The Priory Brewery, from an advertisement of the 1920s when it had been acquired by Jordan and Addington.

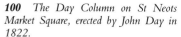

100 The Day Column on St Neots Market Square, erected by John Day in 1822.

John Day did, nevertheless, give St Neots its first street lamp in the form of the tall cast-iron column on the Market Square which was erected in 1822. An oil lamp burned on top of it to begin with, being replaced later by gas lighting.

A remarkable man called George Bower arrived in St Neots in the early years of the century and bought an ironmonger's business. For a time he sold farm machinery and other items but soon became involved in manufacturing gas-making equipment and domestic gas appliances. He sold the ironmongery business and concentrated on his foundry, which was behind the buildings on the south side of the Market Square. He already had a foundry in West Hartlepool which made equipment such as gasholders and retorts for the production of gas, and in his St Neots foundry he made domestic gas appliances. A catalogue of the products he offered for sale, published in 1851, shows pictures of gas fires, elaborate light fittings and some of the first gas cookers that were ever produced. Mr. Bower was a clever engineer but, like the Fourdriniers, he was not a good businessman. He made a quantity of gas-producing equipment for a country in South America and shipped it out at his own expense, even sending a man with it to instruct the new owners on its installation and use. When he failed to extract payment from the country's government he too went bankrupt. Nevertheless the name of George Bower is still remembered as an important one in the history of the gas industry.

101   An advertisement dated 1856 for gas cookers manufactured by George Bower.

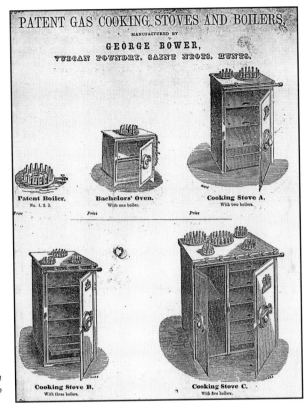

102   The south side of the Market Square, photographed in 1858. The steam engine in the right foreground is believed to have been manufactured by George Bower.

103 The Eagle *public house and Dalby's Brewery at the southern end of Eaton Socon, in about 1900.*

During the first half of the 19th century stagecoach travel was at its peak. Passing through St Neots in 1836 were the *Perseverance* coach travelling between London and Boston, the London to Oundle *Regulator* and the *Old Oundle* doing the same journey. The *Regent* went back and forth between London and Stamford, the *Express* between London and Lincoln and the *Rockingham* between London and Leeds. On a route which crossed the paths of these coaches were the *Eagle* between Cambridge and Birmingham and the *Oxford* between Cambridge and Oxford. In addition there were several mailcoaches which rarely had names but were distinguished by their maroon livery and the Royal Crest painted on them. These coaches all took the loop into St Neots while at Eaton Socon there were even more stagecoaches passing through. By the time traffic from both places had joined up at Alconbury Hill with stagecoaches using the Old North Road, the stretch from there to Norman Cross was the busiest length of road in England. There were estimated to be coaches passing along it at the rate of one every 20 minutes, day and night, and the *Bell Inn* at Stilton, where teams of horses were changed, had stabling for over 300 horses.

One of the few remaining indications of stagecoach travel in St Neots is a sign painted high up on a building on the corner of New Street and Bedford Street. It says 'Hyde Park Corner' and would originally have shown a mileage. Stagecoach drivers sat high up and mileage signs were placed at a high level to catch their eyes, Hyde Park Corner being one of the termini for coaches travelling to London.

Stagecoaches had to pay tolls, like all other road users, but returns for the Southoe tollgate show that one coach at least paid a weekly sum rather than having to pay every trip. The mailcoaches, being on official business, did not pay tolls so tollgate keepers had to listen for the sound of the post-horn and open the gate quickly to let the mails through without stopping, otherwise they risked a heavy fine.

Stagecoach travel was not without its hazards, of course. Being loaded with more passengers on top than inside they were top-heavy, and bad roads or too fast a speed could result in a coach overturning or passengers falling off. St Neots provided an extra hazard of its own because the road by the Paper Mill often flooded—as it still does—and extra horses were then required to haul the coaches through the flood waters. On one such occasion the water was so deep that it invaded the coach and, according to one account, 'all but set afloat two old ladies who were inside'. The writer described their cries of alarm as 'quite affecting'. Another hazard for travellers was the possibility of meeting highwaymen. Although most of the local robbers operated near Stangate Hole, north of Alconbury Hill, there were a few lurking nearer the town. William Emery, the man who recalled the priory gatehouse, remembered his father talking about

two 'desperate characters' called Hitchcock and Stevens, who lived sometimes at St Neots and sometimes at Great Paxton. They hid themselves during the daytime in a field at Crosshall then came out at night to attack travellers and rob them as they passed over Hail Bridge on the Great North Road.

Traders and manufacturers continued to make use of the Ouse and Henbrook for the transport of their goods and raw materials, loading and unloading at the public wharf in Brook Street or at their own private jetties if their properties backed onto the river or brook. In 1850, however, a new means of transport became available with the coming of the railways. The route eventually chosen for the trains of the Great Northern Railway Company passed just to the east of St Neots and the town acquired a railway station, whereas Eaton Socon, which was also eager for a station, never got one.

104 *St Neots railway station in about 1900.*

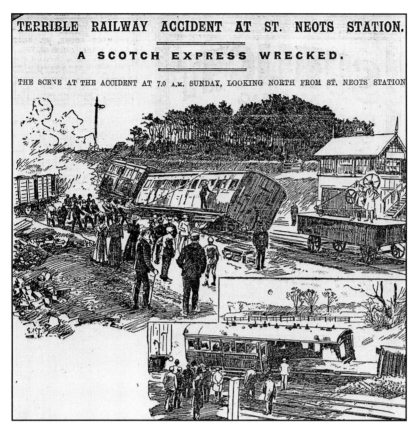

Rail travel was to prove popular with passengers as well as providing quicker transport for goods and, as this popularity was nation-wide, railways gradually ousted stagecoaches. Some local short-distance routes survived for a time, often linking with the railway stations, and these were eventually superseded by horse buses, but the long-distance stagecoaches disappeared forever. The enterprising innkeeper of *The Cross Keys* at St Neots, reluctant to lose the custom of travellers waiting for stagecoaches, ran a coach from his inn to the railway station, claiming that it met every train.

Rail travellers were encouraged to use the trains by being offered special outings to seaside resorts and various annual events. There were excursions to Skegness, Cromer and Great Yarmouth and other east coast places to begin with and by the 1890s trains were taking day trippers even further afield to Scarborough and Brighton. There were trips to London for exhibitions and to Ascot and Epsom for racing. Many local groups took advantage of the special fares offered and as well as works outings there were excursions by local choirs and Sunday Schools.

Train travel was beset by problems too. Sometimes there were not enough seats available and people had to travel in the guard's van. Sometimes trains forgot to stop at stations and there were often delays due to minor accidents or mechanical failure. As well as minor accidents involving slight injuries there were one or two involving fatalities. In 1898 a coalyard worker was killed when taking a short cut across the line near St Neots and the following year a similar rash action resulted in another death near Skew Bridge. The worst local rail accident happened in 1895. A carriage of the 11.30 p.m. train from Kings Cross to Scotland became derailed just outside St Neots station and dragged several other carriages off the line with it. One carriage was completely wrecked and several more damaged, the whole incident creating havoc along the line and causing two deaths and a number of serious injuries. At the inquest on one of the deaths it was stated that a broken rail had caused the derailment and the railway company was severely criticised, in an official report published later, for re-using old rails as an economy move.

Rail accidents were not the only mishaps. The town and the surrounding countryside were constantly under threat from flooding, which happened almost every other year throughout the 19th century. The worst flood was in 1823 and it was described in the local press in these words:

At eight o'clock in the evening of October 30th, when the flood was at its highest, not a house in the town but was inundated to a considerable depth; in many the water ran over the shop counters and in some it was more than five feet deep; indeed in one or two instances it was up to the ceiling ... One poor woman who had been compelled to take refuge

from the flood in the garret remained from Saturday night to Monday morning without food ... persons were rowing about the Market Place in boats and brewing tubs, endeavouring to render aid; and amongst other things swept away by the destructive element a pig-stye was seen floating down the streets ... At Eaton Socon a poor man was rescued from his dwelling in a boat only a minute before his house was overwhelmed.

According to G.C. Gorham the greatest height reached by the water in 1823 was 10ft. 8in. above normal and the parish church, which usually escaped flooding, was two feet under water.

There were other floods almost as severe, such as the one in 1869 when the countryside all around 'had the appearance of an inland sea', and the flood of 1875 when a mailcoach driver was thrown from his vehicle in Cambridge Street and almost drowned. In most years the river rose about 5ft. but in 1894 it rose over 7ft. Houses and shops had to be evacuated by boat and the waters spread over most of Eaton Ford and Eynesbury as well as St Neots.

106   *Floods in St Neots Market Square in 1894.*

107   Mill Lane, St Neots, photographed in 1895 after the hurricane had uprooted several trees.

In 1895 another kind of natural catastrophe caused damage in the town and the villages. A high wind of hurricane force swept through the area on 24 March, uprooting trees, taking tiles off roofs, demolishing chimneys and levelling fences and walls. Part of the stonework of St Neots church roof came crashing down and leading was stripped off. In Mill Lane 37 mature trees were blown down and Mr. Rowley counted about 160 trees uprooted on his property. At Eaton Ford another 36 trees came down and Eaton Socon lost its brewery chimney. Damage was caused to farm buildings at Eynesbury and the river was churned into spray, with fishing huts being blown from one side of the river to the other. Fortunately there was no loss of life but several residents had narrow escapes as chimneys and roof tiles crashed through their homes.

Another constant danger, man-made this time, was fire. Many shops and houses had thatched roofs and fires, once started, could spread rapidly from one building to the next. 1n 1814 a fire, which was reputedly started by men trying to split some wood with gunpowder, set alight a thatched roof in Cambridge Street and 11 houses were destroyed before the blaze was brought under control. A spark from a threshing engine is believed to have started a fire in 1877 which consumed several haystacks near St Neots railway station and there were many instances of smaller fires. St Neots and Eaton Socon both had fire engines but these were inadequate to deal with serious incidents as they relied on firemen who had to be summoned from work, and horses which had to be borrowed as required.

Crime was not a major problem during the 19th century and most of the cases which came to court involved petty theft or poaching, but in 1829 there was a daring bank robbery which hit the headlines. Among several banks in St Neots which were owned by local people was one on the Market Square which was run by William

Foster and his son Josiah, with the help of an assistant called Richard Wise. On 9 July 1829 Josiah and Richard left the premises to take a tea break, locking the door behind them but leaving a large sum of money on the counter and in drawers instead of in the safe. On returning to the bank Josiah Foster found that the door had been forced and the money, which amounted to about £8,000, had gone. Suspicion fell on a man from London called Thomas Hollingshead who had been seen alighting from a coach and later acting strangely on the steps of the bank, together with another man. Hollingshead was arrested and sent for trial but his accomplice was never traced. At the time of his trial in 1830 Hollingshead threatened to implicate others but he gave no names and was convicted on his own, being sentenced to transportation. It was rumoured that a banknote for £500 which had been among the money stolen in the raid was the means by which the robber was found, since it proved impossible to cash it, but no mention was made in the press reports of the rest of the money. It seems very likely that the accomplice made off with at least some of it, and that he was a local man. Someone living in or near St Neots would have known the bank staff's usual routine and would also have known that on a Thursday, which is when the robbery took place, the bank would have been holding more money than usual as it was market day.

A more serious crime than this occurred in the early part of the century which, although it did not happen in St Neots, involved a former resident of the town. John and Elizabeth Bellingham lived in a house on the corner of Huntingdon Street and Cambridge Street and John junior is believed to have been born there in 1776. When the younger John Bellingham grew up he married and worked at various occupations before entering a merchant's office in Liverpool. His job entailed travelling to several countries including Russia, where he negotiated timber contracts. These contracts were not fulfilled, either through Bellingham's incompetence or the failures of others, and the unfortunate negotiator found himself in a

Russian prison. He was eventually released and returned to England an embittered and resentful man, accusing the Russians of having cheated him. For some months he petitioned various government departments and even the Prince Regent, airing his complaints and trying to get compensation for his grievances, but his pleas were ignored. This indifference so enraged John Bellingham that he went to the House of Commons on 11 May 1812 where he shot and killed the Prime Minister, Mr. Spencer Percival. With hindsight one can guess that Bellingham was suffering from persecution mania but no allowance was made for his state of mind at the time, as the crime aroused widespread alarm. No-one had ever assassinated a British Prime Minister before and public feeling was so strong that the culprit's trial was rushed through with unusual haste and John Bellingham was hanged less than a week after the shooting.

108 John Bellingham. A drawing made during his trial.

Nonconformism grew steadily throughout the century. At St Neots the Methodists, who had been meeting in a building in Huntingdon Street, built a new church on the site in 1868. According to the 1851 Ecclesiastical Census they had an average evening congregation of over 600 whereas the parish church only claimed an average attendance of 500. At the Old Meeting House there were another 442 worshippers when the census was taken. This group became known as the Congregationalists and they erected a new church between the Old Meeting House and the High Street in 1889. Baptists had been established in the town since 1810 and were meeting in New Street by 1816. In 1851 the census recorded 294 worshippers at the evening service, and 449 at the morning one. The census also recorded that the Church of Latter Day Saints, popularly known as the Mormons, had a modest congregation of 25. A small Gospel Hall, built in New Street in 1867, served another small group of nonconformists and in 1891 the Salvation Army Citadel was erected on the corner of High Street and Church Street.

At Eaton Socon the 1851 census showed that the parish church's average attendance of 300 was almost matched by the Wesleyan Methodists' evening attendance at their chapel, built in 1850, and at Eaton Ford there was a Primitive Methodist chapel built in 1871. Eynesbury had its Methodists too, but in 1851 the congregation there was only 70 compared with the parish church's 600.

The presence of all these Dissenters in the community was not accepted with tolerance by all the local residents. Mr. Rowley of Priory Hill was described by a contemporary as having 'great zeal for the Established Church' and 'an aversion to the Dissenters'. He resented the fact that the nonconformist preachers, particularly the Baptist minister Mr. Morrell, were better speakers and had more personality than the Vicar of St Neots, and he tried to have the Vicar replaced. Nor was he alone in his objections. In 1815 two St Neots men were accused of disturbing a Baptist meeting by 'driving into the congregation a black dog with a tin saucepan tied to its tail'.

109   The Wesleyan Methodist School formerly in Priory Road, St Neots.

110   *The Methodist Church, Huntingdon Street, in about 1895.*

111   *The Methodist Chapel at Eaton Socon, now converted into flats.*

112 Pupils of the Wesleyan School in 1896.

113 Eynesbury Church of England School, built in 1868.

Both the Established Church and the Methodists founded schools in the 19th century and built premises to house them. The old Charity School became the National School in 1854 and a new school building was erected in Church Walk in 1860. At first it housed pupils of both sexes but later it contained only boys, while the girls and infants used separate premises in Huntingdon Street.

The Methodist School was built in 1858 on land to the north of Priory Road and the building continued in use as Priory Road School until the 1960s.

At Eynesbury pupils were originally taught in a building near The Green, still called the Old School Yard, and by 1818 they had moved to premises in Montagu Street, which still have the old bell-cote on top. They were then moved to a new school next to it which was erected in 1868. In that year there were 80 juniors and 75 infants attending but by 1884 the roll had

probably risen without more teachers being employed as one teacher complained of having a class of over 80 pupils!

Eaton Socon's National School was erected in 1832 to the east of the parish church and it housed 54 boys and 63 girls. Evidently the numbers increased there too because by 1860 the school was found to be too small and a larger building was constructed on the site.

It was not only education which was catered for at this period. The Public Rooms were opened in St Neots in 1855, next to the bridge, and they provided a venue for meetings and concerts. In 1863 the Corn Exchange was built on the corner of High Street and South Street and, although it was designed as an indoor market for farmers, it also catered for concerts and meetings and, after 1887, it housed the Victoria Museum. This museum was set up to mark Queen Victoria's Golden Jubilee and the exhibits, mostly stuffed animals,

114   An engraving of the Corn Exchange in 1863.

were donated by a local doctor, John Jewel Evans.

Other facilities were provided by the Library and Literary Institute, founded in 1881, the Liberal Club, and the Constitutional Club, founded in 1895. The residents of Eynesbury and Eaton probably made use of all the facilities at St Neots but, although neither village had its own purpose-built venue, there was a Workmen's Club at Eaton Socon from 1880, meeting in the school, and at Eynesbury a Reading Room was established in the school there in 1868.

Sport in and around the town, which had been enjoyed in an informal way for many years, was organised into properly constituted and regulated clubs in the late 19th century. Cricket was played by St Neots Wanderers Cricket Club until 1897 and in that year St Neots Cricket Club was formed and began playing regular fixtures on the Common. In 1878 St Neots Football Club was formed and in the 1890s

there was also a St Neots Spa Football Club. A Golf Club, formed in 1890, played games on St Neots Common and later on Hawkesden Leys, there was a Skating Association by 1891 and a Tennis Club from 1898. At about the same time St Neots and Eynesbury combined to form the Quoits Club which played behind *The Chequers* at Eynesbury. By 1893 the town also had a Bicycle Club and a Harriers Club.

Eynesbury had no Cricket Club but football was being played by Eynesbury Hawks F.C. in the 1890s and there was also at one time an Eynesbury Rovers Football Club, but the original club failed and was not re-formed until 1901.

In 1896 both Eaton Socon Wanderers F.C. and Eaton Socon Eagles F.C were playing football. There was apparently a Wanderers Cricket Club as well at Eaton Socon and a Ladies Hockey Club was formed there in 1898.

At the beginning of the century paupers were being accommodated in individual parish

115   Skaters and spectators on St Neots Common and Lammas Meadow in 1889.

DIET SHEET FOR ST NEOTS UNION WORKHOUSE			
	Breakfast	Dinner	Supper
SUNDAY	6 oz bread. One and a half pints gruel.	16 oz meat pudding 12 oz vegetables	6 oz bread and 1 oz cheese or half ounce butter
MONDAY	"	7 oz bread, 1 oz cheese 1 oz onion	"
TUESDAY	"	16 oz suet pudding 12 oz vegetables	"
WEDNESDAY	"	7 oz bread, 1 oz cheese 1 oz onion	"
THURSDAY	"	16 oz meat pudding 12 oz vegetables	"
FRIDAY	"	16 oz suet pudding 12 oz vegetables	"
SATURDAY	"	7 oz bread, 1 oz cheese 1 oz onion	"

116   *The boring diet provided for workhouse inmates.*

workhouses but the Napoleonic Wars brought serious problems for the church authorities which administered them. Men who were killed during the fighting left behind widows and orphans to be cared for, and soldiers who came home injured were often unable to work and sought parish relief themselves. The strain upon the system meant that fewer and fewer people in work were being asked to support more and more paupers. The solution was an Act of Parliament which was passed following a Poor Law Report of 1834. This authorised the establishment of unions of parishes in order to pool resources and to house the poor of all these parishes in one large workhouse. The Report had advocated harsher measures as well, to discourage people from seeking parish relief. In the new workhouses the sexes were to be segregated, food was to be coarser and the inmates given work that was deliberately non-productive.

St Neots Union was formed in 1835 and consisted of 30 parishes, some of them in Huntingdonshire and some in Bedfordshire. A workhouse was built in St Neots Road, Eaton Ford which was designed on the recommended lines with separate blocks for men, women, boys and girls, so that the groups had no contact with each other. The food provided was adequate but incredibly boring, consisting largely of gruel and bread and cheese as the chart shows.

The women worked at household chores while the men were required to break up stones or pick lengths of oakum rope into pieces in order to earn a meal ticket, and the older children were expected to work for half a day too. When the 1881 census was compiled there were 85 males and 52 females in the Union Workhouse, being looked after by a staff of seven. The workhouse master was Matthew Browning and his wife Isabella was matron. Annie Gidding was the schoolmistress and the other staff were a cook, a nurse, a general servant and a porter.

The heartbreak experienced by families forced to seek accommodation in the work-

117 The White House, Eaton Ford, formerly St Neots Union Workhouse.

118 Part of a map of Eaton Ford showing the Union Workhouse (reproduced from the 1901 Ordnance Survey map).

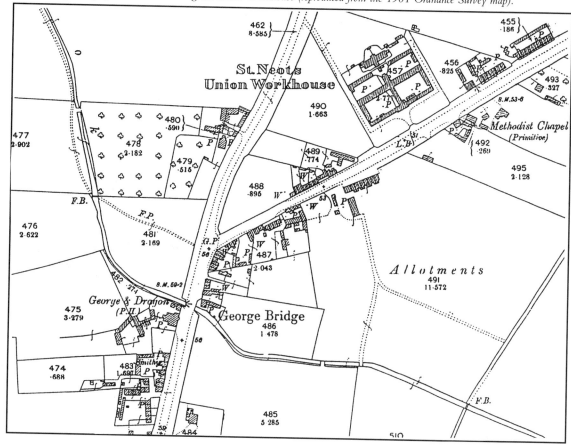

house can be imagined, as parents were separated from their children and from each other, and small toddlers were taken away from mother and father and lost the companionship of brothers and sisters. It must have been equally painful for older people who, finding towards the end of their lives that they could no longer cope at home, were forced to 'go and die in the Union' as one contemporary poet put it.

Despite the various disasters and misfortunes of the 19th century there were several occasions when the town and surrounding villages had cause to celebrate and they did so with enthusiasm, decorating the fronts of shops and houses with festoons of flowers and flags. The first such occasion was in 1814 when the Napoleonic Wars ended. A newspaper report of the period described the decorations and wrote that tables were set up in St Neots Market Square at which 'towards a thousand of the lower class' were fed with roast beef, plum pudding and ale. Hymns and popular songs were sung, accompanied by a local band, and 'rings were formed for dancing'. As the mailcoach arrived its team of horses was removed and a crowd of people pulled the coach round and round the Market Square, watched by visitors from miles around the town. The festivities went on for three days and included public tea parties, a magic lantern show, a ball at *The Falcon* and a firework display.

In 1863 the town was again decorated with flags and festoons to mark the wedding of Prince Edward to Princess Alexandra. Around St Neots Market Square there were banners bearing patriotic messages such as 'God Bless the Queen, Prince and Princess of Wales' and 'May Health and Happiness Crown Their Union'. A procession of children marched down the High Street through a specially erected archway of greenery, accompanied by the Eynesbury Volunteer Band, and in the evening there were fireworks and other illuminations together with an enormous bonfire on the Market Square. Children were given special teas in their schoolrooms, pony races were held on the Common and there was a shooting contest for members of the St Neots Detachment of the First Huntingdonshire Volunteers.

Queen Victoria's Jubilees in 1887 and 1897 were celebrated in similar fashion, with the latter event being commemorated by the addition of lamp brackets and a flagpole to John Day's column on the Market Square. There were races for adults and children, the usual tea parties and a procession of decorated vehicles, including bicycles.

A different sort of procession took place in 1895 when St Neots Spa was opened. A spring of medicinal water had been discovered issuing from the ground by the Paper Mill bridge and there were hopes that St Neots could be devel-

119 A photograph taken in 1863 on the occasion of the wedding of Prince Edward and Princess Alexandra, showing the archway erected at the east end of High Street.

120 *A street party in Russell Street, St Neots, to celebrate Queen Victoria's Diamond Jubilee in 1897.*

121 *Procession of decorated boats to mark the opening of St Neots Spa in 1895.*

oped as a spa town. A tap was fixed from which glasses of water were sold and the water was also bottled and sold under the name of 'Neotia'. The official opening was celebrated with a procession of decorated boats from the Paper Mill bridge to the town bridge and a company was formed to promote the project. According to reports the water had a particularly foul taste, which may explain why the ambitious plans for its exploitation were eventually abandoned!

Throughout the town and the villages many changes occurred as new buildings were erected and old ones demolished. As well as buildings already mentioned there was a police station and magistrates court, built in New Street, and a number of industrial premises in Bedford Street including a large corn mill, a maltings, an iron foundry and a gas works. Houses for the working families went up in East Street, Russell Street and Shaftesbury Avenue and houses for the well-to-do were built in Avenue Road and Kings Road.

At Eynesbury there were new houses in Luke Street, Buckley Road and Silver Street while at Eaton Socon some of the older houses were replaced along the Great North Road, although there was less new building there. In School Lane at Eaton Socon the 'Cage' was constructed in 1826 to serve as an overnight prison for wrongdoers.

The Census Returns from 1801 onwards show that there was a steady increase in population in all areas and that most of the adults, and some of the children, were employed in either agricultural work or in domestic service. Until the end of the century Hiring Fairs were held at St Neots each year to which men and women came to offer their services to prospective employers, most of whom were looking for farm workers or servants. The Paper Mill was another major employer, as were the breweries, and there was a Brick and Tile Works at Eynesbury. There was also a parchment works at Eynesbury and a number of leather workers at St Neots. In all areas there were bakers, butchers, shopkeepers, tailors, dressmakers, drapers, grocers, carpenters and blacksmiths, plus a few specialised workers like the ink-mixer

122   A hiring fair taking place on St Neots Market Square in about 1890.

123   19th-century trade advertisements.

and the umbrella mender. Evidence of the stagecoach era was revealed by the presence of coach-builders and repairers, saddlers and harness makers, mostly at Eaton Socon and Eaton Ford. At St Neots in 1851 the population was just over 3,000, an increase of about a thousand over the 1801 figure, and at Eynesbury the population doubled between those years from 575 to 1,233. The Eaton Socon figures are difficult to calculate because they included the hamlets within the parish but the population had probably increased there, too.

One of the most interesting documents recording life in 19th-century St Neots is the letter written by William Emery to which reference has been made several times. Mr. Emery recalled the demolition of the buildings on the Market Square, which appeared on the 18th-century map, in these words:

When I was between seven and fourteen years of age the Butchers Shambles were standing upon the Market Hill, there was also the Stall Geer House and several Tradesmen's Shops which were all let. The Principle [sic] People living round the Market Square, having constantly before their houses such numerous indecent scenes committed under the Butchers Shambles and the Butter House that they resolved upon pulling them down and clearing the ground and laying it quite open. Mr. William Peppercorn, farmer at Hardwick, and his son, William Alexander, engaged to plough the Market Hill up and level it and they began to plough it on a Monday morning with a strong and large plough and eight horses and found it very hard work.

We are not told what the 'indecent scenes' were and they may not have been much more than rowdy behaviour. The removal of the buildings seems unlikely to have solved the problem, judging from the fact that similar activities are still going on nowadays!

Chapter 8

War and Expansion—1900 to 1995

At the beginning of the 20th century the Manor of St Neots changed hands. Mr. George Fydell Rowley, whose family had lived at Priory Hill House since the end of the 18th century, bought the lordship from the Earl of Sandwich. Much of the Sandwich property was already in Mr. Rowley's hands, acquired when the Earl's financial problems caused him to sell it in 1848, and when the lordship was purchased Mr. Rowley confirmed his position as the dominant local character. 'Character' is probably the right word to use as he is known to have been somewhat eccentric. He used to walk about the countryside dressed very shabbily and was often mistaken for a tramp. He also hated motor cars so visitors to Priory Hill House were expected to arrive on foot or by horse-drawn carriage, or they were not admitted. By 1910 the Rowley holdings included Manor Farm and Tithe Farm at Wintringham, Love's Farm on the Cambridge Road, Monks Hardwick Farm and the Paper Mill with its adjoining meadows. This was in addition to numerous acres of land, cottages and houses, Islands Common and Hawkesden Leys, and the tolls of St Neots Market.

124 *Priory Hill House, St Neots, was the home of the Rowleys. It was demolished in 1965.*

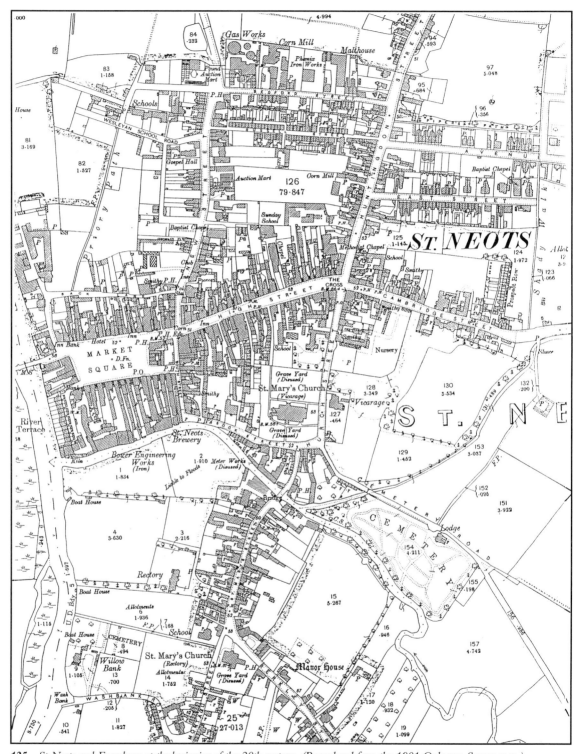

125   *St Neots and Eynesbury at the beginning of the 20th century. (Reproduced from the 1901 Ordnance Survey map.)*

Life in the town and villages changed very little in the early years. Photographs taken between 1910 and 1920 show that the locality was still provided with many small family shops and businesses and that traffic consisted mainly of horse and cart. By 1910 there were a few cars on the roads but most of the wheeled transport consisted of bicycles and motor cycles. Even these created little hazard to pedestrians as a speed limit of 20 miles per hour was in force in 1914 which applied to all vehicles within the urban area and there was a 10 miles per hour limit for cars within the town itself. Directories for 1900 echo the pattern of compact communities with small traders serving local needs while almanacs from the same period reflect the flavour of the time in their advertisements. One proclaimed that Mr. J.Kurr made pork pies and sausages daily at his premises in the High Street and Mr. Fred Kendall of Church Street stated, in another advertisement, that he sold 'Prime Pickled Pork' and 'Smoked Pig's Cheeks'. W.E. Davies offered 'Suits to order from 31s. 6d.' while H.R. Chick of New Street sold ready-made suits at a slightly cheaper price and his goods included 'Gent's Knicker Hose'. 'Dressmaking in all its branches' was 'executed with neatness and despatch' by Mrs. H. May, and W. Edwards was the agent for 'Tread Easy', 'Cinderella' and other brands of footwear. The chemists offered a wonderful collection of cure-alls including 'Rowlett's Worlds Blood Mixture' which not only conquered pain but also cured 'Eczema, Pimples, Tumours, Cancers, King's Evil, Ulcers, Blotches, etc'. Two notable local photographers, Mr. Phillips and Mr. Jenkins, also advertised, the latter boasting that he was 'Patronised by Lady Esme Gordon and the Clergy and Gentry of the Neighbourhood'.

126   *The Market Square in about 1900.*

127   Barrett's Corner, Market Square, in about 1900.

128   The south side of High Street in about 1900. The entrance to Church Walk is at the centre, to the left of the boy with the pram. The timbered building shown in illustration 46 lay behind the brickwork beyond.

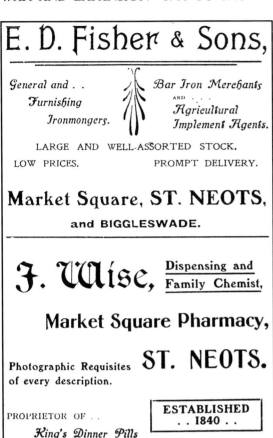

129-130   Advertisements for Market Square shops, and High Street shops, from an almanac for 1916.

The majority of local men were employed as agricultural labourers, as in previous years, and the women in domestic service, but there were others who sought to improve their employment potential by enrolling in evening classes for short-hand, typing and commercial arithmetic. From 1910 onwards a number of local people took advantage of a scheme which encouraged emigration to Canada where the government was offering land to immigrants which could be paid for over a period of 20 years and in some cases cottages were also provided.

In their leisure time local residents enjoyed sports and amateur entertainments. The river, always an important factor in the life of the neighbourhood, was alive with activities in the summer months with boating on it, swimming in it and fishing from its banks. In the winter the river froze over and there was skating on it. Lammas Meadow, beside the river, was also flooded and allowed to freeze to provide safer skating for all.

The yearly festivals were celebrated as in previous centuries, with Village Feasts at which there was dancing and sports, and on May Days there were other customs. In St Neots and Eynesbury small children paraded from door to door carrying a circular garland in which hung a doll, covered with a cloth. On receipt of a penny the cloth would be raised to show the 'May Lady'. At Eaton Socon maypole dancing was revived in 1905 and continued to take place for several years, attracting huge crowds of spectators.

131   Girls carrying the May Garland with its doll at Eynesbury in about 1932.

This placid way of life was shattered in 1914 by the outbreak of the First World War. Many local men volunteered for the armed services and left for France and other areas. Reservists were called up and the men from Huntingdonshire as well as Bedfordshire joined the Bedfordshire Regiment, later re-named the Beds. and Herts. Regiment. Initially, however, the rush to enlist was slower than expected. Newspapers of 1914 and 1915 carried advertisements stating that the 5th Beds. needed recruits urgently and there were also requests for 'well-educated men' to join the East Anglian Cyclists Battalion. Several men from St Neots and Eynesbury joined this oddly-named body and were stationed for most of the war at Skegness. Their duties involved patrolling the coast from Scarborough to Hornsea, presumably to watch out for possible invaders. Although the Hunts. Cyclists were issued with 10 cars in 1915, the rank and file continued to patrol on their 615

bicycles. They were never much in the public eye and they were reputedly known in the Scarborough area as 'John Bull's Lost Regiment'.

As time progressed there was considerable pressure to enlist and those seeking exemption from military service had to appear before a tribunal. The pressures were obviously social as well as official, judging by a paragraph which appeared in the *St Neots Advertiser* in 1915 which stated, 'William Nicholson asks us to say that the only reason he has not joined the Army is because of a varicose vein'.

Although farm workers were usually given exemption many of them joined voluntarily, creating a shortage of labour for local farmers. In the late summer of 1915 it was reported that a number of soldiers had been released to help with the harvest and the re-opening of schools after the summer holidays was delayed to enable schoolchildren to help, too.

Soldiers from other parts of the country were stationed at St Neots during the war. An artillery unit made the town its base and stored its large guns in a field to the north of the town, near the grounds of Priory Hill House. For many years this field was known as 'The Gun Park' or 'Artillery Field'. Bad weather, however, threatened to bog the guns down and they were transferred to St Neots Market Square. What the situation was on market days is not recorded.

The war years reduced the number of traffic offences, perhaps due to vehicles being requisitioned, but the number of thefts increased. Most of these involved thefts of food or livestock which suggests that local people were suffering from shortage of provisions. Minor crimes such as assault and poaching remained at the usual level but a slight increase in juvenile crime was reported, perhaps due to the absence of a father's restraining hand. Most of the youngsters' crimes would be considered minor by today's standards—playing football in the street or scrumping apples—although there were also a few cases of more serious theft.

Local residents supported the armed forces in many ways. Ladies knitted items such as gloves, scarves and socks for soldiers in the

132   *A May Day procession through Eaton Ford in about 1910, on its way to The Green at Eaton Socon.*

133   *Dancers on Eaton Socon Green in about 1910, waiting to perform round the maypole.*

134   Pupils of Eaton Socon school in 1904 with their headmaster, Mr. Huckle.

135   St Neots decorated with flags to celebrate the Coronation of King George V in 1911.

136 *Artillery on St Neots Market Square during the First World War.*

trenches and a number of concerts and other events were organised to raise money for other comforts. At Eaton Socon Mrs. Butler's house became a convalescent home for wounded soldiers, and many local women took over jobs which had previously been done by men.

One event which brightened the gloom of the war years was the opening of the Pavilion Cinema which was set up in the Corn Exchange at the corner of South Street, St Neots, by installing a projector and building a large screen at the back of the stage. To begin with a few short films were shown and there was also live entertainment to complete the programme, but as time went on more films were shown.

The end of the war in 1918 was celebrated in the customary fashion with street parties and a procession. War memorials were erected later to commemorate the local men who had given their lives. The memorial at St Neots has a small garden to itself in the churchyard. Eynesbury's' memorial also stands in its churchyard but at Eaton Socon the commemorative column was set up on the Green.

Life was destined never to return to its pre-war style, however, because the social climate had changed forever. Those who had previously worked in domestic service had enjoyed more interesting occupations during the war and were reluctant to return to the restricted world of service, while those who had experienced the responsibilities of leadership in the armed forces were loth to take up employment in more menial positions. Higher wages had to be offered and farm workers' pay rose from 23s. 6d. a week in 1913 to 40s. in 1920.

137   The War Memorial on Eaton Socon Green, photographed in the 1930s.

Overtime was paid, with special rates for Sunday working. Although these increases were welcomed by farm workers at the time they were eventually to lead to many of them being put out of work as farmers invested more in machines as a way of saving labour costs. Domestic servants were also in demand and a housemaid could ask for £30 a year instead of the pre-war average of £17. The local gentry families began to curtail their staff accordingly and the middle-class households learnt to do without servants altogether.

From 1922 to 1925 new Council houses were built in Cromwell Gardens, Cambridge Gardens and Ferrars Avenue and more housing was added in the 1930s along Potton Road in Eynesbury and in the Crescent area of St Neots. Some private houses were also built and these, like the Council houses, were for renting as very few people at that time could afford to buy houses.

Traffic increased after the war, particularly along the Great North Road. A traffic survey carried out in August 1922, covering a seven-day period, recorded over a thousand motor cycles and even more bicycles. There were 1,846 motor cars on the road and together with other forms of motor transport such as vans and lorries this made a total of 2,289 compared to the number of horse-drawn vehicles which was 273. It was mostly long-distance traffic, however, and within the town of St Neots the traffic consisted of a mixture of cars, bicycles and horse-drawn carts.

Fires were almost as much of a problem in the early 20th century as they had been in the 19th. In 1905 a mill on the Market Square at St Neots, next to the brewery and owned by the same firm, caught fire and threatened other adjacent buildings. Paine's other mill in Bedford Street was closed so that workers from there could come and help remove stocks to safety, but although the brewery and most of its stock were saved, an outhouse in the yard and a quantity of bottled beer were consumed by the fire. At one stage the flames shot higher than the brewery chimney and neighbouring traders were so alarmed that they also began moving their stock and valuables. Mr. Wise the chemist took paraffin out of harm's way and Mr. Fisher at the ironmongery jettisoned his gunpowder into Hen Brook! St Neots fire brigade attended with their hose-cart but it required the assistance of firemen from Huntingdon, Bedford and Sandy to extinguish the flames.

In 1909 the other flour mill in Bedford Street was itself almost completely destroyed by fire. It had been built in 1846 for John Medlock and bought by William Paine in 1865. Fire brigades from Huntingdon and Sandy again came to the rescue of the local brigade but when the fire was finally put out only the shell of the building remained and it was not considered practical to restore it. The following year a new mill was built on the site, part of which, including the old campanile-style tower, now forms the centrepiece of a housing complex.

In 1912 a serious fire destroyed most of the paper mill and tackling it proved yet again too much for St Neots fire brigade. Even with the help of the usual neighbouring services a great many of the buildings on the site ended in ashes but rebuilding was started almost at once and the mill was operating again in 1913.

In 1929 it was the Pavilion Cinema which suffered. The fire there reduced the old Corn Exchange to a smouldering shell, although fortunately most of the cinema equipment was saved. The interior was rebuilt and what was left of the exterior was repaired so that the cinema was able to re-open the following year.

By far the most serious fire was the one which swept through Eaton Socon church in 1930. Despite the valiant efforts of local brigades the entire interior of the church was consumed, destroying the medieval carved benches and the fine roof timbers. Residents described hearing the roaring of the flames and the resounding crash as the bells fell through the tower. When

the fire was finally out all that remained was a shell, with some of the walls in imminent danger of collapse.

There were suggestions that the best solution was the demolition of the remains and the construction of a smaller church but this idea was rejected in favour of total restoration. Professor Albert Richardson, later Sir Albert, was commissioned as architect and his designs proved so effective that when the church was re-dedicated in 1932 it looked very much the same as it had done before the fire. Nowadays it is difficult to realise that Eaton Socon church is not as old as it looks.

138 *The aftermath of the fire at Paine & Co's flour mill in Bedford Street in 1909.*

139   The paper mill fire in 1912.

140   The damage caused by the fire at the paper mill in 1912.

141   Eaton Socon church on fire in 1930.

In the years before the war a series of Acts had been passed to replace the old Poor Laws, providing payment for the unemployed and pensions for the elderly, so the Union Workhouse at Eaton Ford was no longer required. It was officially closed in 1929, although it was later used for a time as an old people's home. Health care improved generally with regular visiting of schools by doctors and dentists, and district nurses being provided.

In 1935 one local nurse was faced with a challenging task. In Ferrars Avenue, Eynesbury, Mrs. Miles gave birth to quadruplets, three boys and a girl, having expected to produce twins! The care and competence shown by Dr. Harrison and District Nurse Mailing ensured that all the babies were safely delivered and were well and healthy. It was the first time that such a multiple birth in this country had resulted in all four babies surviving and the Miles family became famous. The babies' progress was followed for many years by the national press and their upbringing was made easier by the sponsorship of a baby-food firm who provided food supplies and equipment. The family moved to a house in St Neots, on the corner of New Street and Tan Yard, where the public were able to come and peep at them through the nursery window on payment of a shilling. They became known as the 'St Neots Quads' in spite of having been born at Eynesbury.

Earlier in 1935 St Neots had been celebrating the Silver Jubilee of King George V and Queen Mary, with the usual street parties and processions, but the following year the King died and was succeeded by his eldest son. King Edward VIII was never crowned, however, and the Coronation festivities which enlivened the local scene in 1937 were for George VI and Queen Elizabeth.

All these events were soon overshadowed by the outbreak of the Second World War in 1939. As before, local men—and women, too, this time—enlisted in the forces and preparations were made to defend the country. The proximity of airfields at Great Staughton, Kimbolton, Great Gransden, Graveley, Toseland and Tempsford led the local authorities to expect German air raids and among the first bodies set up were the Observer Corps and the Air Raid

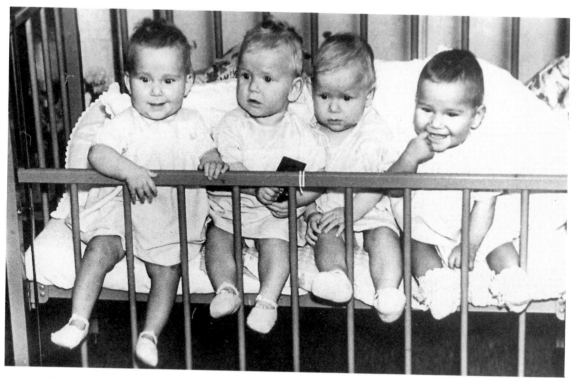

142-43   The 'St Neots Quads', photographed in the 1930s, when they were about one year old and as toddlers.

144   *A procession through Eynesbury in 1935 to celebrate the Silver Jubilee of King George V.*

Precautions Unit. At Eaton Socon an Invasion Committee was set up in 1941 to organise Civil Defence, fire-fighting and food distribution in the event of an invasion. Tank traps were placed in readiness beside the road across St Neots Common and a pill box, which can still be seen, was built on land in Ware Road over-looking the Common.

Fortunately these precautions proved unnecessary and the various bodies were called on to do little more than hold themselves in readiness. The only bombs which fell in the locality are thought to have been jettisoned by a lone German bomber returning from a raid elsewhere. High explosive bombs fell in a field to the north of Mill Lane in St Neots and several incendiary bombs were dropped further east in an area which is now part of the Longsands Estate but which was only farmland

at the time. No-one was killed or injured in the attack and the only damage was to crops. The occupant of one of the Mill Lane houses which back on to the field where the bigger bombs fell is reported as saying that she was glad she had called her cat in just before they were dropped!

Some damage to houses and other property was caused by plane crashes. An aircraft attempting to land at Toseland hit a house and crashed, killing its crew, and another aircraft crashed at Crosshall. On another occasion a fight between a German bomber and a Hurricane resulted in the German plane crashing on to power lines at Eaton Socon and a policeman trying to put out the fire which followed was electrocuted and killed.

Apart from the departure of men and women into the forces the major change to the local scene was the arrival of a number of evacuees. Children from London and other towns and cities were sent away to country areas for safety and the first evacuees from London arrived in St Neots early in the war. They were taken to the playing field at Eaton Socon where prospective hosts selected those to whom they would give a temporary home. A second contingent arrived in 1944 as a result of the V1 flying bomb attacks and they were also taken in by local residents. The experience of leaving home for the first time must have been a harrowing one for the children concerned and, as one news report stated, 'the pathetic sight of these mites ... standing with

their few possessions in the midst of strangers, bravely trying to keep a stiff upper lip, moved to tears a number of W.V.S. ladies who were looking after them.'

Some of the children settled down to rural life quite well but others returned home, either through their own homesickness or because their parents missed them, with the child population changing frequently as more evacuees arrived.

The end of the war in Europe in 1945 was celebrated with the usual parties and fireworks, festivities which were repeated when Japan surrendered. More names were added to the local war memorials, although thankfully

145   *St Neots Market Square during the Jubilee celebrations, 1935.*

146   The pill box in Ware Road overlooking St Neots Common, built during the Second World War.

not as many as after the First World War, and life began to get back to normal despite the fact that food rationing had to continue.

Flooding had affected the locality throughout the first half of the century with floods in 1908, 1918 and 1940 but the worst inundation occurred in 1947, causing havoc over a wide area. Food had to be delivered by army amphibious vehicles to marooned families at Eaton Ford and a swan was seen pecking at the window of a partially submerged house. The height to which the waters rose that year can be seen marked on a stone set into a wall in South Street.

During the 1940s and '50s plans were made to move families out of London and house them in other towns, together with industries and offices to provide work, and St Neots was one of the towns which entered into an Overspill Agreement with London boroughs. From 1960 onwards houses and business premises were built on the outskirts of St Neots and Eynesbury and from 1965, when Eaton Socon and Eaton Ford were absorbed into St Neots, this expansion also spread across the river. The result was that between 1960 and 1970 the population of

St Neots grew from about 5,000 to over 20,000 and the area acquired a new look. The town centre changed, too, as old buildings were demolished, or had their frontages updated, to make way for new shops and several local landmarks disappeared. Priory Hill House, no longer occupied by the Rowley family, was knocked down to make way for housing and its grounds became a public park. The buildings of the former Priory Brewery were reduced to the barley kiln and part of the maltings, their place being taken by the Priory Centre and a new public library.

In 1964 the historic and picturesque town bridge disappeared to be replaced with the present concrete structure and the osier beds beside the river were later drained and landscaped to form the Riverside Park.

Part of Islands Common was tidied up and marked out to provide pitches for rugby and hockey to be played there as well as cricket when St Neots Sports Association was formed and other sports pitches were provided in Priory Park. New schools were built to cater for the children of new residents, including two secondary schools, and during the 1960s the former Wesleyan School in Priory Road was

147   An aerial view looking west along Henbrook towards the River Ouse, during the floods of 1947.

demolished and the church school in Church Walk abandoned in favour of newer premises.

In 1968 the town lost its cinema when the Pavilion closed down but by then various societies had been formed which provided entertainment and leisure activities. St Neots Players performed plays at Longsands School and The Stablehands presented Shakespeare in the yard of *The Kings Head* in South Street while musical entertainment was supplied by the Choral Society and the Music Hall Society. From 1948 there were also the annual Carnivals to enjoy.

Since 1970 the town has grown steadily in spite of the ending of the Overspill Agreement. The reorganisation of local government boundaries in 1964 caused the disappearance of Huntingdonshire and the old county became part of Cambridgeshire, a move not received favourably by many older residents. Improvements to river management means that the town no longer suffers from flooding although the riverside grass areas lie under water most winters. The re-routing of the A1 to the west and the construction of a by-pass to the south means that there are fewer problems with traffic in the town.

In 1995 the former Magistrates Court in New Street, St Neots was opened as a town museum, its old cells being among the attractions. This museum will be a valuable asset to the amenities of the town and will help to reveal to residents and visitors alike the many interesting and varied events which have featured in St Neots' past.

148 *St Neots bridge as it was before being rebuilt in 1964.*

149 *The Priory Centre, built in the 1970s on the site of the Norman priory.*

Bibliography

Abbreviations

C.A.S. Procs.	Cambridge Antiquarian Society Proceedings
C.R.O. Bed.	County Record Office, Bedford
C.R.O. Hunt.	County Record Office, Huntingdon
L.Mus. Bull	Longsands Museum Bulletin
Norris	Norris Museum and Library, St Ives, Cambs.
St Neots L.H.Mag.	St Neots Local History Magazine
St Neots L.H.S.Coll.	St Neots Local History Collection
Trans.C and H.A.S.	Transactions of the Cambridgeshire and Huntingdonshire Archaeological Society

General

Bigmore, P., *Bedfordshire and Huntingdonshire Landscape* (1979)

Bushby, D., *From River Farm to Modern Suburb—Eaton Socon and its Church* (1994)

Godber, J., *History of Bedfordshire* (1984)

Gorham, G.C., *History and Antiquities of Eynesbury and St Neots* (1824)

Royal Commission on Historical Monuments, *Huntingdonshire* (1926)

Tebbutt, C.F., *St Neots* (1978)

Victoria County History of Bedfordshire (1904)

Victoria County History of Huntingdonshire (1932)

Young, R.E., *St Neots and Eynesbury* (1978)

Young, R.E., *The History of St Neots for Children* (1994)

Chapter 1

Archaeological maps and records, St Neots area, Cambridgeshire County Council

Fox, C., *Archaeology of the Cambridge Region* (1923)

Rudd, G.T. and Daines, C., 'Late Iron Age settlement at Crosshall, Eaton Ford', *L.Mus Bull*, No. 4. (1973)

Rudd, G.T. and Daines, C., 'Roman burials from Duloe Road, Eaton Ford', *C.A.S. Procs.* Vol. LXIII (1971)

Rudd, G.T. and Daines, C., 'Romano-British settlement at Eynesbury', *C.A.S. Procs.* Vol. LXI (1968)

Tebbutt, C.F., 'Excavations at Eynesbury Coneygeare', *Trans. C. and H.A.S.*, Vol.V (1937)

The Viatores, *Roman Roads in the S.E. Midlands* (1964)

Young, R.E., 'Roads in the St Neots area', *St Neots L.H.Mag.*, No. 21 (1993)

Chapter 2

Addyman, P.V.,'Late Saxon settlements: the village or township of St Neots', *C.A.S.Procs.* Vol. LXIV (1973)

Addyman, P.V., 'Saxon settlements and Norman castle at Eaton Socon, Beds,' *C.A.S.Procs.* Vol. LVIII (1965)

Bushby, D., 'Anglo-Saxon finds in Avenue Road, St Neots', *St Neots L.H.Mag.*, No. 28 (1995)

Chibnall, M., 'St Neots Priory', *C.A.S.Procs.* Vol. LIX (1966)

Lethbridge, T.C. and Tebbutt, C.F., 'Excavations at the castle site known as The Hillings, at Eaton Socon, Beds.', *C.A.S.Procs.* Vol. XLV (1951)

Lethbridge, T.C. and Tebbutt, C.F., 'Huts of the Anglo-Saxon period', *C.A.S.Procs.* Vol. XXXIII (1932)

Mawer, A. and Stenton, F.M., *Place Names of Bedfordshire and Huntingdonshire* (1926)

Morris, J., *Domesday Book, Bedfordshire* (1977)

Morris, J., *Domesday Book, Huntingdonshire* (1975)

Chapter 3

Alexander, M., *Medieval burials at 25-23 Market Square, St Neots* (1994)

Forscutt, L., 'Lowering St Neots Church Floor 1847', *St Neots L.H.Mag.*, No. 23 (1994)

Gross, C., *Select Cases from Coroners Rolls* (1896)

Jervoise, E., *Ancient Bridges of Mid and Eastern England* (1932)

Letter from William Emery, Proby Collection, Norris

Morris, J., *Domesday Book, Bedfordshire* (1977)

Morris, J., *Domesday Book, Huntingdonshire* (1975)

Record Commission, *Rotuli Hundredorum* (1818)

Reed, L. and Goodwin, H.W., 'Eynesbury Hardwick', *St Neots L.H.Mag.*, No. 2 (1983)

Tebbutt, C.F. and Chibnall, M., 'St Neots Priory', *C.A.S.Procs.* Vol. LIX (1966)

Young, R.E., 'Royal Visitors', *St Neots L.H.Mag.*, No. 16 (1990)

Young, R.E., 'The Lost Village of Sudbury,' *St Neots L.H.Mag.*, No. 6 (1984)

Young, R.E., 'The Priory Gatehouse', *St Neots L.H.Mag.*, No. 13 (1988)

Chapter 4

Arbitration Award for St Neots 1564, Copy in Author's own collection

Gorham, G.C., *Supplement to the History of Eynesbury and St Neots* (1824)

Hamilton Thompson, A. (ed.), *Visitations of Religious Houses in Diocese of Lincoln* (1914)

Ladds, S.I., 'An Old Door from St Neots', *Trans. C. and H.A.S.*, Vol. V (1937)

Manor Court Rolls for St Neots, 16th Century, C.R.O. Hunt.

Tebbutt, C.F. and Chibnall, M., 'St Neots Priory', *C.A.S.Procs.* Vol. LIX (1966)

Young, R.E., 'St Neots Priory in 1505', *St Neots L.H.Mag.*, No. 27 (1995)

Chapter 5

Hearth Tax Returns for Eaton Socon 1674, C.R.O. Bed.

Hearth Tax Returns for Eynesbury and St Neots 1671, C.R.O. Hunt.

Kingston, A., *East Anglia and the Great Civil War* (1897)

Lee, R., *Bedfordshire and the Civil War* (1986)

Parish Records for Eaton Socon, C.R.O. Bed.

Parish Records for Eynesbury and St Neots, C.R.O. Hunt.

Proby, G., 'Protestation Returns for Huntingdonshire', *Trans. C. and H.A.S.*, Vol. V (1937)

Wedgwood, C.V., *The King's War 1641-1647* (1958)

Wills, D., 'The Battle of St Neots', *St Neots L.H.Mag.*, No. 6 (1984)

Chapter 6

Andrews, C.B. (ed.), *The Torrington Diaries* (1954)
A First Directory of St Neots 1792 St Neots L.H.S. Coll.
Birch-Reynardson, C.T., *Down the Road* (1875)
Bushby, D., 'John Wesley and St Neots', *St Neots L.H.Mag.*, No. 13 (1988)
Bushby, D., 'The Severed Head', *St Neots L.H.Mag.*, No. 18 (1991)
Copeland, J., *Roads and their Traffic 1750-1850* (1968)
Defoe, D., *Tour through the Whole Island of Great Britain* (1724-7)
Goodwin, H.W., 'The Bellfounders of St Neots', *St Neots L.H.Mag.*, No. 3 (1983)
Harper, C.G., *Stagecoach and Mail in Days of Yore* (1903)
Inclosure Act and Award for St Neots 1770-1, C.R.O. Hunt.
Valuation, St Neots 1809, Norris
Young, R.E., 'The Hawthorn Hunter of Southoe', *St Neots L.H.Mag.*, No. 3 (1983)
Young, R.E., 'Two Local Breweries', *St Neots L.H.Mag.*, No 12 (1987)

Chapter 7

Bates, A., *Directory of Stagecoach Services 1836* (1969)
Bushby, D., 'Off to the Seaside', *St Neots L.H.Mag.*, No. 17 (1990)
Bushby, D., *St Neots Sporting Years 1896-1901* (1983)
Bushby, D., 'Some Local Railway Accidents', *St Neots L.H.Mag.*, No. 6 (1984)
Bushby, D., 'The 1851 Ecclesiastical Census', *St Neots L.H.Mag.*, No. 7 (1984)
Cambridge Chronicle, 'Celebrations of Peace 1814', *St Neots L.H.Mag.*, No. 27 (1995)
Census Returns St Neots and Eynesbury 1801-81, C.R.O. Hunt.
Forscutt, L. and Hawkins, J., 'John Bellingham', *St Neots L.H.Mag.*, No. 1 (1982)
Forscutt, L., 'Royal Wedding Celebrations 1863', *St Neots L.H.Mag.*, No. 22 (1993)
Hadley, J., 'The St Neots Railway Accident 1895', *St Neots L.H.Mag.*, No. 3 (1983)
Hawkins, J., 'Fire! Fire!', *St Neots L.H.Mag.*, No. 3 (1983)
Knight, F. (ed.), *Letters to William Frend from the Reynolds family 1793-1814* (1974)
Poor Law Union Records St Neots, C.R.O. Hunt.
Reed, L., 'The Floods of November 1894', *St Neots L.H.Mag.*, No. 10 (1986)
Wells Almanac for St Neots 1896
Young, R.E., 'St Neots Bank Robbery', *St Neots L.H.Mag.*, No. 22 (1993)

Chapter 8

Basson, G., 'In Search of the Hunts Cyclists', *St Neots L.H.Mag.*, No. 9 (1985)
Basson, G., 'More Exploits of the Hunts Cyclists', *St Neots L.H.Mag.*, No. 13 (1988)
Basson, G., 'Traffic Census 1922', *St Neots L.H.Mag.*, No. 19 (1992)
Brice, P. and others, *St Neots Urban District Council 1894-1974* (1974)
Forscutt, L., 'Rowley Family Holdings in 1910', *St Neots L.H.Mag.*, No. 19 (1992)
Peppitt, H., 'The St Neots Quads', *St Neots L.H.Mag.*, No. 28 (1995)
Reed, L., 'The Outbreak of the First World War', *St Neots L.H.Mag.*, No. 15 (1989)
Selley, S., 'Crime in St Neots in the First World War Period', *St Neots L.H.Mag.*, No. 19 (1992)
Selley, S., 'When the Church Bells Ring', *St Neots L.H.Mag.*, No. 5 (1984)
Tebbutt, C.F., *Huntingdonshire Folklore* (1951)
Tebbutt, C.F., 'St Neots in Wartime 1939-45', *St Neots L.H.Mag.*, No. 10 (1986)
Young, R.E., 'Employment in St Neots 1910-20', *St Neots L.H.Mag.*, No. 14 (1988)
Young, R.E., *St Neots in Old Picture Postcards* Vols. 1 and 2 (1983, 1994)

Index

Pages on which illustrations appear are shown in **bold** type.